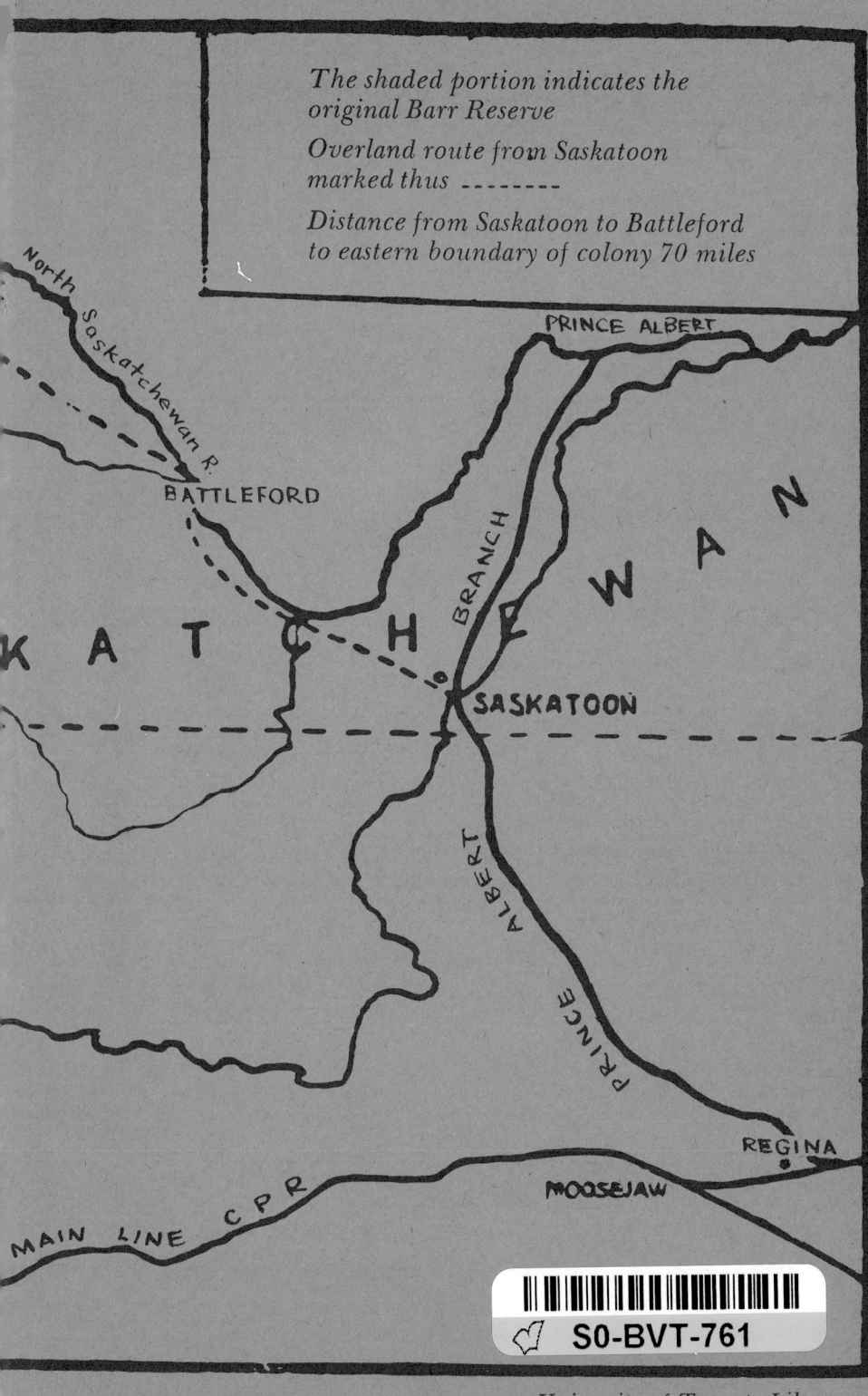

The shaded portion indicates the
original Barr Reserve

Overland route from Saskatoon
marked thus --------

Distance from Saskatoon to Battleford
to eastern boundary of colony 70 miles

North Saskatchewan R.

BATTLEFORD

PRINCE ALBERT

K A T C H E W A N

BRANCH

SASKATOON

ALBERT

PRINCE

REGINA

MAIN LINE C P R

MOOSEJAW

All Silent,
All Damned

All Silent, All Damned

The Search for Isaac Barr

HELEN EVANS REID

Toronto
The Ryerson Press

© Helen Evans Reid 1969

SBN 7700 0273 0

Library of Congress Catalog Card Number: 70-84986

Grateful acknowledgment is made to the
following for permission to quote from
copyrighted material: CURTIS BROWN LIMITED,
LONDON, *Cecil Rhodes, Colossus of Southern
Africa* by J. G. Lockhart and C. M. Woodhouse.

*Every reasonable care has been taken to trace
ownership of copyrighted material used in this
book. The author and publisher will welcome
information that will enable them to rectify any
errors or omissions.*

PRINTED AND BOUND IN CANADA BY THE RYERSON PRESS TORONTO

For William who has always believed

Acknowledgments

Since the memory of the elderly is keen but capricious and recall tends to telescope time, I have relied, with one notable exception, on personal accounts for opinions, descriptions and anecdotes only. For facts, in the search for Isaac Barr, I have relied on original documents, official reports and newspaper accounts published at the time—not in retrospect.

I acknowledge with gratitude the assistance given me by officers of the Diocese of Huron, Diocese of Tennessee and Diocese of Michigan; by the Reverend Dr. Frank Peake, Department of History, Laurentian University, and Miss Joyce Harrison, Office of the County Auditor, New Whatcom, Washington; by Miss Ruth Murray, University of Saskatchewan Library, Saskatoon; by M. Pierre Brunet, formerly of the Public Archives of Canada; by Dr. Robert Blackburn, Chief Librarian, University of Toronto; by the late F. Ivan Crossley, the late Harry Messum and the late The Honourable Mr. Justice J. L. McLennan; by the curators of records in Salisbury, Rhodesia, Oxford University and Lambeth Palace; by the innumerable clerks in all the counties of Nebraska, Ohio, Washington, Tennessee and Michigan and the vital records offices of the provinces of Ontario and Saskatchewan.

I especially thank those owners of private collections of Barr memorabilia: Alec Messum, Thomas Parr, Helen Thompson and Samuel Noyes.

Without the help of all these, this book could not have been written.

H. E. R.

Contents

Illustrations

But as you by their faces see,
All silent and all damn'd!

Peter Bell, Wordsworth
First edition, 1819

The Beginning

This book is the result of an outright prevarication. Mine. It is an attempt to write my way out of a trap I fashioned for myself.

As an infant I had dwelt briefly in the land of the Barr Colonists, that rich strip of the valley of the North Saskatchewan River that lies south of the river itself and stretches west from North Battleford, Saskatchewan, to about thirty miles across the border into Alberta. As a child I had come to know one Barr Colonist well, to listen to the tales of blizzard and hardship, recalcitrant cows and the lonely prairie nights; of the long wagon trail and the crude sod shacks; tales which, mellowed in Irish wit, became stories of high adventure, of humour and pathos, with a credibility gap that widened over the years.

I had always vaguely felt that I should record for Canada the story of the party of two thousand persons "of good British stock" who, under the leadership of the Reverend Isaac Montgomery Barr, left their tidy English homes and shops, their commuter trains, morning papers, bowlers and umbrellas and journeyed five thousand miles by sea, train and wagon train to settle in a block on the empty prairies of the Canadian Northwest, to farm on government-grant lands almost two hundred miles beyond the railhead. They brought with them money, firearms with which to face the frontier, pianos and a vast inexperience in the agricultural arts to survive as the Barr Colony of 1903.

1

A brief note in a University of Toronto publication early in 1963 stating that the library had acquired the Mavor Papers relating to the Doukhobors and the Barr Colony made my decision.[1] These papers were the personal correspondence of Professor James Mavor of the Department of Political Economy, University of Toronto.

Concerned about the success of block settlements in Canada, and faced with the need for making a decision whether the government should continue to sponsor schemes to establish emigrants in groups in the new land, the British parliament had set up a committee under Lord Tennyson (the poet's son) to investigate the problems encountered and to recommend a policy for the future.

Professor Mavor was sent west in 1905 to visit both Doukhobor and Barr Colony settlements, to investigate conditions and on his return to appear before the committee to present his findings. Some of the correspondence on which he based his evaluation is contained in the papers as well as a sharp exchange of letters between the professor and the Reverend George Exton Lloyd, chaplain to the Barr Colony, who expressed annoyance with the Mavor Report, both by letter and in interviews in the public press.

I was persuaded that I should record the stories, and now, before too many of the personal accounts precious to historians were lost.

At the library my request to read the Mavor Papers produced surprise and reluctance. The chief librarian explained that under the terms of the gift they were to be made available for use by "serious students of history." Did I qualify? I told him of my intention and of my Barr Colonist, Ivan Crossley; of how the words, vivid, warm, flecked with humour or hesitant with tenderness (for Ivan had a slight stutter), tripped off his Irish tongue. With a pen in his hand he would be paralyzed and silent, but tape recordings would capture the essence of the telling, I was sure.

Was this really history? And what did I plan to do with the tapes?

It was then that I told the lie: complete, precise, definite, as new to me as to him. Facing him squarely and in spite of the sense of awe I have always felt in the presence of librarians, I said, "But I *am* a serious student of history. I am going to write an article about the Barr Colony and a book." I was committed.

We struck a small bargain, the librarian and I. In exchange for the privilege of reading the papers the university would be given the tapes as a sort of "living history" for their Canadiana collection.

In the next few weeks I read all I could find about the colony: the several books that have been written about it, the accounts in the historical journals and in the local newspapers of the time, when Barr and his colony were hot news, and then I left for Western Canada to make the recordings.

Kelowna, British Columbia, that mid-May was hot and dry and beautiful. The Okanagan orchards had long since bloomed and the Ogopogo had again failed to appear in the lake. I spent four days listening to Ivan Crossley talk about the colony with only an occasional word from me to stimulate the flow. Then abruptly one morning he said, "You know, the Barr Colonists are holding their sixtieth reunion next month and Pierre Berton* will be there."[2]

The reunion and the personality were bound to attract some public interest. An article on the Barr Colony would be timely and just might help me to recover the cost of the tape recorder and the long train journey to the West. With the gathering a scant six weeks away, I realized the deadline for the manuscript was that very day. Steeped as I was in colony lore, and with Ivan's words sounding in my ears as I played back the tapes I had made, I was ready to write, and I did—all night long. As dawn broke the next day I dispatched a modest piece by airmail to *Maclean's*, Canada's national magazine. Actually it did not appear in print for six months.

When it did, the uncompromising title, THE CLERICAL CON MAN WHO HELPED SETTLE THE WEST, spread above my words so shook me that I did what I had never done before. I read, after publication, something I had written. There was no question; they were my words based on all the accounts

---

*Celebrated writer and TV personality.

I had studied and all the stories I had listened to, checked and double-checked for source up to that date and then offered in good faith.

Why I had not seen the fallacy I do not know unless it was that, enchanted by the stories, I had ceased to remain protectively critical. Almost from the day he enters medical school a doctor is taught to protect himself from error by looking with distrust on vague opinions, with doubt on all statistics. But I had been misled. There, plain and clear, was the flaw in the reasoning:

If, as all the accounts suggested, Barr had "conned" and defrauded his colonists, taking their money without return and profiting from their hardships, why did he continue up to the colony with them? If he had raked in their money before he left England, and certainly before they left Saskatoon, why did he not bolt from there?

For months I thought about this discrepancy. I went back to the historical records, and for the first time I became acutely aware of such phrases as "it is suggested," "tradition says," "believed to have been." Freely translated, these mean the author doesn't know, hasn't tried or has been unable to find out.

By this time I had lost interest in the colony, except as an expression of the man who had initiated the whole movement: Isaac Montgomery Barr. Who was he? What had led him to embark on this venture which was later to be, for him, a total personal disaster? What had become of him after he disappeared, his honesty questioned, his name ridiculed in ribald song and angry slogan?

To reconstruct from a search of the records in the public domain the bare chronological facts of a life so recent is not difficult. To discover in the process a personality with all his dreams and discouragements, his talents and frailties, his triumphs and losses, his loves and hatreds is to know his worth and understand his bitterness.

I have written hundreds of letters, searched through public archives and private correspondence and actually followed Barr's trail back and forth across Canada and the

United States. I have travelled to four countries on three continents. He had once described himself on a document as "a travelling man" and indeed he was.[3]

By thinking constantly about what I have discovered the ties between seemingly unrelated small facts have become clear, either to prove or disprove a doubtful point or start a whole new line of enquiry.

There has also been the tedious but rewarding task of checking the apparent trivia. For example, all the books about the colony and most of the articles, including mine, said in effect, "It was a late, cold spring." Actually it just seemed that way to the unprepared travellers, inappropriately clothed and accustomed to only an occasional sight of snow even in midwinter. The Dominion Meteorological Service states that for Saskatoon and North Battleford the temperatures were *generally above average* for the dates on which the colonists were in those areas, though there were a few brief cold snaps.

Or consider the matter of the SS *Lake Manitoba* on which the colonists sailed. She has been variously described in accounts of the Barr Colony as being "an old ship," "an old converted troop ship," "an old ship used to carry horses to the Boer War." In fact she was launched just twenty-one months before she took aboard the migrants; and her fitting would not have been completed for some time after her launching. She was a very new ship.

These points are trifles in themselves but they have a use; they identify the source from which the historian or the travelling scribe drew his material.

But for the Barr Colony scheme Isaac Montgomery Barr would have remained an insignificant parish priest "who flitted across the pages of Canadian church history,"[4] never remaining for any length of time in a charge and frequently a source of dismay and embarrassment to his superiors.

He did, however, in a few short months organize and transport a group of two thousand persons, with all their household goods, to Western Canada to open up a vast tract of land in the valley of the North Saskatchewan where they flourished and enriched the land and the life of the early settlers. And though his colonists, once there, repudiated his leadership, they and their descendants still refer to that part of the country as the Barr Colony and speak of themselves with pride as Barr Colonists.

Newspapers noting the death of Isaac Barr stated that at one time he planned a colonization scheme in South Africa with Cecil Rhodes and that it was abandoned because of Rhodes' death. This item fixed the time that Isaac would have had to be in Africa—the time of the Boer War. I reasoned he just might have been with the Canadian troops and so I asked the Canadian Department of Veterans Affairs for his war record. There was none. But an alert clerk came up with a short paragraph from the record of a Harry Montgomery Baird Barr, who gave as his next of kin his father, Isaac M. Barr. The paragraph ended with the statement that when Harry died in Africa, his mother received his medals in Windsor, Ontario. So Isaac had been married!

One of the historical accounts said: "Not known to have been married." When I met Mrs. Wetton, author of *The Promised Land,* considered to be one of the more authoritative accounts of the colony, I asked, rather cagily I thought, for I already knew, if Barr had ever been married. "Never!" she replied.

To find a record of the event without knowing the year, the city in which it took place or even the name of the bride seemed impossible. I pursued Barr from parish to parish that he occupied in the 1870s, begging the current incumbents to search their early pastoral registers for any mention of the name Barr. Months later came a find. A kindly priest, after hours of painstaking effort, discovered the baptismal record for a child of the Reverend Isaac M. Barr and his wife, Eliza T. Barr. At last I had a name—Eliza T.

I chose five years before that date as the period during which the marriage could have taken place. I looked again and again, all the time suspecting the Windsor area although I searched the central registry for every county in Ontario over a wide spread of years. Nothing.

Three years later, reading the memoirs of the Reverend George Exton Lloyd, who had accompanied the colony to Canada, I came across a reference to a Reverend Canon Hurst, who recalled that Barr had been a summer student with him in a parish in Canada. It was one of those small, seemingly unrelated facts that made the story whole.Within a few days I had found out the parish where Canon John Hurst had served in 1870, and there indeed, in Windsor, was the record of the marriage I had given up hope of ever finding.

Where records differ, only after considering all the known facts can one decide which statement to accept as valid. For example, on one document dated August 10, 1870, Isaac gave his age as twenty-two years, that is, he was born in 1848; on another dated June 25, 1900, he stated his age was fifty years, that is, he was born in 1850; on yet another, January 18, 1937, six weeks before his birthday, his age is given as eighty-eight years for a birth year of 1848.

The date finally chosen as most likely was March 2, 1847, on the word of his son, and because it was compatible with the time of arrival of his parents in Canada. The baptismal records in his father's first parish, Oakville Trafalgar, could not be located; in fact it is doubtful if they still exist. The Province of Ontario has no record of the birth; it would be surprising if it had, for this was long before the time of central registration.

I had decided when my hero had been born. Now, in the best biographical tradition, I addressed myself to the problem of finding out where.

A Sense of History

"Mr. Barr was himself a Canadian. Born in Halton County, Ontario, he was, it is claimed, the son of a Church of Scotland minister" began *The Coming of the Barr Colonists* in the Annual Report, Canadian Historical Association, 1926. It seemed quite simple though I should have been warned by the phrase "it is claimed," which had neatly relieved the author of any responsibility for verification. As it happened, he was right.

I started from there. The Registrar General of Ontario regretted he had no birth records covering this early period. Surely, I thought, a minister would have had his own son baptized. I must search the baptismal records of the Presbyterian churches of the time in Halton County.

Presbyterian is a broad term, or was then, covering the Presbyterian Church, the Auld Kirk, the Church of Scotland and, naturally, several other variations, for the Scots are a stern and uncompromising lot. Which churches had been present in Halton County as early as 1845? Did they still exist? Had they become part of the United Church in 1925? Where were the records now? Transferred to that body or to another church which continued outside the union? Were the records still extant? And how could I hope to find him when I had no idea of his father's given names?

I began by writing all the present Presbyterian churches in the county—and there are many—with a spectacular lack of success. The ages were wrong or the records had been

8

transferred or were non-existent. From the files in the archives of Victoria, the United Church College at the University of Toronto, I learned which congregations had ceased to be Presbyterian but this offered little help.

Then one morning at Knox College Library I made my first find.

RECORDS OF THE PRESBYTERIAN CHURCH IN CONJUNCTION
WITH THE CHURCH OF SCOTLAND IN CANADA.

Appendix to Synod meeting September 15, 1847

Mr. William Barr, a Licentiate of the Presbytry of Glendermot [Ireland], in connection with the Presbyterian Church in Ireland, admitted by the Presbytry of Toronto, as a Probationer, within their bounds.
1848 Wm. Barr Hornby and Trafalgar.[1]

WILLIAM BARR! Hornby! Halton County!

A few days later I visited that tiny village. Unfortunately the postmaster was new; he had been there only three years. There was no Presbyterian church in Hornby, he said, but there was a boarded-up and unused church about a mile to the east. Somehow I knew this had to be it. I had looked for this place for four months, pestering the busy clergy, a moderator, archivists, elderly men who had once been deacons in little rural congregations. As I wandered through the small surrounding cemetery, pulling back the turf that overgrew the flat gravestones I became more and more convinced. The dates inscribed were right. The birthplaces recorded were the counties of Northern Ireland, Tyrone and Donegal.

Actually I was looking for a special grave, for from another source halfway around the world I had learned that Isaac's mother had been buried in the churchyard where his father preached. Back and forth I criss-crossed the little plots but the stone I sought I could not find.

Discouraged, I went from farm to farm in the neighbourhood asking the same questions at each house. Was this the

Barr church? Did they know where the Barr farm had been? Nothing. At last I met one old gentleman who eyed me silently, his face impassive, while I asked again. After much canny questioning of me he admitted it was the site but not the original church. Then taking me down a roadway he pointed to a spot in an adjoining field and said, "That's where the Barr house stood. Log it was. Got used as a chicken house later. Been gone about ten years. Moved it to the next farm." His father had bought the place from William Barr and my informant had lived next door for seventy years.[2]

More determined than ever, I returned to the little churchyard digging at every depression to uncover the buried stones. Frustrated, discouraged, convinced but still unable to prove my point, I turned to leave. I had noticed a large lilac bush in the centre of the neatly trimmed yard. The unclipped base was a tangle of suckers and bramble. I pulled the heavy branches apart and saw the inscription:

In memory of

CATHARINE

Wife of

Rev. William Barr

who died Apr. 30 1857

AE 35 y'rs

A NATIVE OF DONEGAL IRELAND

Jesus haste oh haste and take me
Let me to thy joys aspire
Now I know thou'll ne'er forsake me
On thy bosom I expire

I had found Isaac's birthplace. Now for the records.

The history of this little parish is one of transfers, association with other congregations, non-union in the 1925 merger, and now well-tended closure. If early records exist, I cannot say where.

Isaac was born here. He had said so,[3] and now I knew
that this was where his parents had lived. The distance between the exact location of the farm and the supporting
document was eight miles; the distance in time was a hundred and seventeen years.

There had been two good reasons for celebrating. It was
Saint Valentine's Day, 1848, and in the little village of
Streetsville, in the Province of Canada, Michael Lindsay of
the Township of Trafalgar and the Reverend William Barr
had just closed a deal for the transfer to Barr of some forty-
nine acres of land ten miles to the west, at Hornby. The land
agent would be one witness and the other—it seemed natural in the chill wind and wet slush of mid-February—
Michael Castor, the local innkeeper.

Made this fourteenth day of February in the year of our
Lord one thousand eight hundred and forty-eight by and
between Michael Lindsay, of the Township of Trafalgar in
the County of Halton . . . Province of Canada, Yoeman, and
William Barr of the Township of Esquesing in the said
County of Halton, Presbyterian Minister, Whereby the said
party of the first part for and in consideration of the sum of
three hundred pounds of lawful money of the Province of
Canada . . . did give, grant, bargain, sell, alien, assign, transfer, enfeoff, convey and confirm unto the said party of the
third part, his heirs and assigns all the parcel or tract of land
situate in the said Township of Trafalgar, containing by
measurement 49 acres . . . being composed of . . . the west
half of lot number fifteen in the eight concession, excepting
one acre at the westerly angle of the said lot . . . which has
been conveyed by Michael Lindsay to Gilbert Adams. . . .[4]

As the little pile of "lawful money" lay on the table the
document was completed. Then when each signed in the
appropriate place and host Castor had given his witness,
they toasted the bargain in Irish whiskey, the best in the
house. Warmed by the fire and the good spirits, content
with the day's business, William Barr and Michael Lindsay
climbed into the buggy and headed home.

The Reverend William Barr was a native of Strabane, County Tyrone.[5] He graduated from Belfast University[6] and "preached in connection with" the Presbyterian Church of Ireland.[7] In 1846, when he was thirty-one years old, he emigrated to Canada bringing with him his wife, Catharine Baird Barr, pregnant with their first child.

Catharine, seven years younger than her husband, had been born in Donegal into a proud and well-to-do family steeped in naval tradition. On her mother's side, the Montgomerys were descendants of Huguenots who had escaped the massacre of St. Bartholomew's Day.[8] Her father was a Presbyterian clergyman and William had been his assistant.[9]

Like most immigrants to Canada from the British Isles they almost certainly sailed from Liverpool and would have been six or eight weeks bound for New York or Quebec. The choice lay between the long voyage up the St. Lawrence to Quebec and on by ship or stage to York (Toronto), or the shorter voyage to New York, then up the Hudson and by canal to Oswego and on to York.

Travellers brought with them their own food for the trip, sufficient, say, for seventy days: corned beef, flour, oatmeal, ham, some live fowl, wine, perhaps a little rum, potatoes and other vegetables.[10] And packed in the hold were furniture, bedding and clothing. Though William Barr's was not a large household, supply was difficult in the new land and it would take considerable money to provide for the family he hoped to have.

Why he chose Hornby is obscure. Perhaps it was because homesteaders from counties Tyrone and Donegal were already there; the Lindsays, Hemstreets and Fords; the Maddens, David Forrest[11] and Ephraim Ervin and his wife Jane. The settlement was a tiny collection of homes, a blacksmith's shop and a small store, that outlined the crossroads where the post office stood. The east and west road allowance separated Esquesing Township to the north from Trafalgar to the south. In later years Hornby boasted six pubs and there was a saying abroad that "there were two places no Liberal dared to speak, hell and Hornby!"[12]

The young preacher and his wife were welcome in this little community of the fiercely Presbyterian. In those times an established settler would take in the newcomer and his family until he could establish his own home on his own farm. Thus it was that in Esquesing Township, Halton County, on a farm near the village of Hornby, Isaac Montgomery Barr was born on March 2, 1847. By the time the family moved to the Barr farm just across the road in Trafalgar Township, the second child, John, had also arrived. The new home stood on an abrupt height to the west of a small valley where a little creek twisted and tumbled. Built of hand-hewn logs cut from the great trees on the place, squared and morticed at the corners, it was roofed with shingles shaped by hand.[13] The house was about thirty by twenty feet and was centred by a huge fireplace opening on the kitchen-dining room for warmth and cooking. The minister's small parlour was at the rear. From it a narrow stairway of wide pine planks, led to the three small rooms above where the family slept.[14]

To his family Barr was a stern man and a demanding father. He expected the children, who arrived with a predictable regularity every two years, to perform the tasks assigned to them with promptness and efficiency and if they failed to do so his wrath was fierce and sudden. As soon as he was able, Isaac helped with the chores.

The family kept a few cows and chickens and cultivated a large garden, more for convenience than to supplement the family living, for though the salary of a missionary was small and uncertain, William Barr managed his wife's money well.[15, 16] Catharine had brought a large dowry to the marriage and on the long journey to Upper Canada a rich trousseau came with her: linens, clothing, fine shoes of the softest kid. During the twelve years or so of her marriage she "made down" all these garments into clothing for the children.

The few private schools of the time, situated mostly in the larger towns like York, were run by masters with indifferent qualifications who received the going rate of one hundred and fifty dollars a year—if they could get it. In country areas the pioneer pedagogue collected what he could from fond parents and boarded round with the families he tutored.[17]

This was not good enough for William Barr. He schooled his children himself from the books that crowded his parlour shelves: Shakespeare and the English poets; history —mainly British; translations from the ancient Greek; and other solid books extolling the good Presbyterian virtues and warning against sin. By the time Isaac was ten, he was fluent in Latin and Greek and, if his mathematics was wobbly, he could at least read and speak considerable Hebrew.[18]

There was no need to travel much beyond this close-knit little community. For the missionary's family, life was centred and complete in little Hornby. For Catharine, it was strange and lonely and hard, with the child-bearing, the cold, the reluctant fires, water to be hauled, household laundry to be scrubbed by hand, soap to be made, food to be preserved, sewing and mending to be done. Church services were held each Sunday in their own home, for the small congregation could not yet afford a kirk. Mail and supplies were there in the village. So was the first of the pubs; but frivolity was not encouraged. Weddings and funerals were community affairs with much of the food supplied by the neighbourhood ladies. When nearby farmers gathered for a barn-raising their wives and children spent the day preparing a great picnic feast to be eaten when the building was up. The evening was spent in dancing, with frequent trips to the nearby woods for stinging draughts of Irish whiskey.

Around Hornby, the Province of Canada was filling up. Transportation had improved. In 1850 it was announced that a stage would leave Kellogg's, Colborne Street, in York daily except Sunday for Streetsville. The first passenger train in Canada started May 16, 1853, from York for Aurora, drawn by the *Lady Elgin*, a locomotive named for the Governor's lady. Two hours later it reached its destination, thirty miles away. All along the right of way, people coming from far and near on foot, on horseback or, if the roads permitted, by buggy, had gathered to watch this historic event.[19]

Isaac's father was often absent from home, sometimes overnight, as he went about his parish duties. In the long evenings, when there were no lessons, when the lamps were lighted and the smaller children were in bed, Catharine Baird Barr would sing in a deep contralto voice the songs of her people, the old Irish ballads, and would tell stories of her family and Ireland, of Wellington and the young Victoria.[20]

There was magic for Isaac in the very name of his township, Trafalgar. His great-uncle had fought in that famous battle as a surgeon in Nelson's flagship, and was still living.[21] As Catharine repeated the thrilling stories of naval encounters, ship against ship, tattered sails, powder monkeys, red-hot cannon balls and flaming victory, the small boy listened and history became a reality.[22]

His father always ended each school lesson with a recitation from the Shorter Catechism; before long, so automatic had the exercise become that Isaac could produce the perfect response to every question while, uninterrupted, he steered his frigate into glorious battle or schemed with Clive to hold India for his queen. Then, still dreaming, he climbed to the room he shared with his brother Jack. The dour Presbyterian minister remained below, seated at his table, while his wife placed before him a kettle of hot water, a bowl of hard sugar and a glass. Handing him the decanter and a pewter spoon with a ring in the handle she watched solemnly while he mixed and drank his nightcap.[23]

Isaac was ten when his mother died in childbirth, leaving William Barr with two sons, Isaac and John, and three daughters, Catharine, Margaret and the newborn infant, Sarah Jane (Jennie). The loss of his wife was not only a grief to the missionary but an inconvenience. He badly needed someone to look after his children, all under eleven.

Shortly before the family moved to Dungannon, near Goderich, William Barr married Sophia McKidd, sister of a Presbyterian minister. There were three children in the second family. The last was a boy, Willie. Isaac was very fond of this half-brother and over the years they remained fast friends in spite of the great difference in age. Isaac missed his mother's gay presence. He was moody and lonely. He talked about the Bairds in Ireland a great deal and began corresponding with them.

For Sophia too this must have been a trying time. Her husband was often away from home on his missionary rounds, leaving her alone to care for the seven children and a farm that had to be made to provide for their needs. Isaac, who of all the children remembered his mother best, was unhappy, which of course produced some friction. He felt that Sophia was a cruel stepmother[24] and Sophia regarded the two boys as "wild and undisciplined." They were always in trouble and their father vented his "vile temper— and it was a terrible temper"—on them.[25]

Now William Barr was a great Orangeman, Irish Presbyterian that he was, and a great preacher too. "On Sunday morning he would take a good shot of whiskey, Irish whiskey if he could get it, then march up to the kirk and preach steadily for two hours at least. He seemed to get all wound up and he would give that sermon all he had. He would seem to be carried away with his own eloquence."[26]

A childhood friend of the Barr children, Gavin Hamilton Green, has left a description of what life was like for a boy growing up in Dungannon at that time:

There was a maiden lady of the name of Green who kept a private school in Dungannon. She was always on the lookout for pupils. The building where this private school was held was on Main Street . . . across the road from the old PRINCE OF ORANGE which had for a sign Prince William on a horse.

On Monday morning dressed in brown duck trousers and in linen coat, with a penny in my pocket to pay the teacher (penny a day being the rate), I started for my first day at school.

There were lots of girls. I remember there were three or four girls named Barr. These girls were daughters of Reverend Barr, Presbyterian minister, who preached in the old Barr church as it was called in those days, situated about a mile from Dungannon on the road to the Nile.

I learned a few things; I learned to play hookey but did not know it was wrong . . . I began to learn some street talk and a few cuss words. . . . The Reverend Barr did the school inspecting.

Dr. McKay as the medical officer . . . came to inspect our health. We all had to march out into the yard, pull up our shirt sleeves to our elbows. Doctor walked past, examined our hands and arms. If we had itch we were put to one side. Well the biggest part of the school had itch and had to go home. Some of the aristocratic girls from the village cried when they had to come across to the itch side. The cure was stay home from school for three weeks, be washed every night in a tub of salt water—then rub a stinking brown salve all over. David and I hollered and yelled.

My parents being Scotch Presbyterians we went to the old Barr church. My father used to take David and me and mother when she could, but as she generally had a baby to nurse at home these times she seldom went. . . . We had been taught that little boys who go to church would go to heaven when they died, and little boys who did not go to church would go to the bad place, where there was a lake of fire and brimstone. We felt very sorry for the little boys that did not go to church on Sunday . . . [we] were always ready to go to insure escaping this burning lake.

One day as David and I were on our way to Barr's church we found a big horseshoe. A horseshoe was worth a penny. Two cents was some money to us boys in those days. Well, we did not want to hide the horseshoe along the fence as someone might get it so we decided to take it to church with us. I had on a white linen coat and I put the horseshoe under it, so no one would see it. When we got as far as the village, it was getting quite heavy and it was hard for me to keep it under my coat, so I said to David, "Let us go to the English Church," which was in the village. So to the English Church we went. We then carried the horseshoe home and hid it in the henhouse, and took it with us on Monday morning when we went to school, and sold it to the blacksmith. . . .

We said nothing about the English Church business to our parents . . . [but] David and I decided that in the future we would attend the English Church. We liked to see the preacher in his white gown in the low pulpit and in his black gown in the high pulpit. We liked the singing. People smiled and looked pleasant at one another, while in Mr. Barr's

Church people always looked so sour and sad. We were
always afraid to look round in Barr's church.... A neighbour
woman visiting at our place said to Mother, "I saw your two
little boys at our church on Sunday." Well, Mother being a
stiff Presbyterian, soon stopped that performance, and back
to Barr's church we had to go. Well, David and I decided to
go to heaven with Mr. Jones' church instead of Mr. Barr's
church. We were getting along splendidly, had the litany of
the service nearly all off by heart ... I ... [had] decided to
become an English church preacher.
    We put in a protest . . . that if we could not go to Mr.
Jones' church we would not go to any; that we would go
to hell with the other boys that did not go to church. . . .
Mother wanted to know where I learned the word "hell."
I told Mother I had heard Barr the minister say "hell" in
church. But that did not save me. . . . David and I felt very
badly as we knew Mr. Jones, he often went fishing and hunting with our father. He was a jolly fellow, would laugh,
smoke, play cards, etc.

Just as children today imagine themselves spacemen,
Isaac's contemporaries played at being preachers:

Then I began to preach every afternoon! Saturday about we
boys used to go to our respective homes to play. These visits
generally ended in a fight, the visitors calling the hosts nasty
names until they were out of hearing. When they came to
our house to play I always preached. I preached in the
stable using boxes for pulpits, Mother's white nightgown
for the first part of the service, and a black silk shawl of
mother's for the high pulpit part. I must have been very
eloquent as the congregation always remained and listened
to my discourse. I recited the litany part and what I
preached, I guess, were parts of sermons I had heard at both
the English and Presbyterian churches. My sermons were a
cross between the two, flavoured strongly with hell fire and
brimstone. After I found out that the bad place was called
"hell" I seemed to like to say it better than "the bad place."
It was shorter and had the punch. My congregation liked to
hear me say "hell fire and brimstone." I told them that if
they were bad boys and did not say their prayers at night,
told lies, said swear words, or made faces at the school-

master when he wasn't looking, that was where they would all go; or if they whistled on Sunday or cut a stick with a jack-knife, or caught grasshoppers or ladybugs on Sunday instead of going to church they would go to hell sure. I seemed to get so much hell fire and brimstone in my sermons that I was frightened of my own preaching. I know I always ended the preaching with these words, "Let your light shine before all men," to let the congregation know to get their collection ready. I took up the offering myself, which generally consisted of pieces of slate pencils, buttons, bits of candy, pieces of coloured glass, sometimes a bit of cake. Once I got a copper.[27]

The Barrs had always led a frugal life and with the money from his first wife's dowry William bought a farm for each of the boys, "to settle them down properly."[28] It didn't really work. Both Jack and Isaac promptly sold the farms and left, Jack to disappear to the West, and Isaac for Ireland to visit his mother's people.

His stay in Ireland was one of the most significant periods of his life. "The Bairds were the ones that most strongly influenced my father. They gave him that feeling of personal involvement in British history, the desire to do something himself to further the development of the Empire." He spent endless hours just listening to his great-uncle, Captain John Baird of Trafalgar fame, who so appreciated his audience that when he died at the age of one hundred and three years he left the boy a modest inheritance of a thousand pounds[29] and the belief that he too had a part to play in the great tide of British expansion, that he too would be an empire builder.

The Trouble With Bishops

"Every generation of Barrs had one who wagged his head in a pulpit"[1] and when Isaac returned to Canada he set about becoming that one. With his strong Presbyterian background it is surprising that he chose to become an Anglican priest. Geography may have been a factor; the infant Huron College, London, was the nearest theological school. But perhaps he too had found the Anglican flock in Dungannon more friendly and the threats of the lake of fire and brimstone weakened by repetition. Ritual and panoply, more prominent here than in the austere religion in which he had been raised, had always appealed to him. All his life Isaac was impressed by officialdom; he seemed never to question what was said provided it was said by "an official" with the proper bureaucratic title. He may have felt more comfortable with the structured hierarchy of the Anglican Church. He himself said, "I came under the influence of some leading Anglican clergymen so I switched."[2]

In any case, "the records of Mr. Barr's stay at Huron College consist of his fees paid for room and board and tuition during the years 1868 to 1871 in the general ledger of the college. He attended before the establishment of the University and before the time of the keeping of official records, apart from the general ledger stating what gentlemen were under the tuition of the college staff."[3] Nothing more.

When the college opened, candidates for admission were examined in Latin and Greek grammar, and were expected to read and translate these languages readily. They were also examined in arithmetic, algebra up to quadratic equations and in the earlier books of Euclid. Each was required to declare that, were he successful, he would subscribe to the laws of the college and diligently prosecute all the studies and perform all the duties assigned to him.[4] This declaration alone was to cause Isaac trouble later.

Luckily for Barr, the entrance rules had been relaxed just before he arrived, so that he was required only to pass a test in Greek and Latin grammar and in at least one Greek and Latin author. Father Barr's training had been sufficient and he was enrolled. Any student who was not already a university graduate had to spend one year in the general course followed by two years in theological studies.

Set in fourteen acres of parkland, the college building consisted of a large family house purchased in an estate sale. To this had been added a students' wing of three storeys. On the ground floor of the new wing were three rooms divided by folding doors permitting the whole area, on occasion, to be opened up to form one large hall. The floors above provided studies for the students and dormitories.

It must have been cold in the building in winter, for minutes of the council meetings at the time showed prolonged concern with double-sash or storm windows, furnaces to be installed, and the terms of employment of a new matron, a Mrs. Fox, who offered to board the students for $2.50 a week each, but refused to stoke either the furnace or the stove in the students' sitting room.

Unless their parents happened to reside in London, students were required to live in the college, where they paid board and forty dollars a year for room rent, fuel, tuition and the use of the library. Each supplied his own furniture and lighting—generally by coal-oil lamps.

A cap and gown "of approved pattern" were to be worn at all times both inside and outside the college grounds.[5] Under a heavy winter coat or over it? Either way, Isaac with his stocky figure, crowned by a college cap, would have been a memorable sight as he plodded his way through the

London snow alone, or frequently in the company of his classmate and close friend, Evan Davis.

The students usually accepted on those occasions when they were invited by the principal "to his residence to meet members of his family and such other friends as he might ask to meet them for the double purpose of imparting religious instruction and affording them opportunities for social intercourse."⁶ The principal's house was warm and comfortable, and if the conversation lagged he was always ready to suggest a topic for debate.

While he was a student at Huron College Barr met Dean Isaac Hellmuth, later to become his bishop. This remarkable man, a Jew born in Warsaw and educated in a rabbinical school, had been enrolled in the University of Breslau when he was only sixteen. While at the university he became converted to Christianity, and after a year of doubts and tensions finally informed his father that he could no longer continue his education as a rabbi. His father disowned him. Assuming his mother's maiden name, Hellmuth left Germany and proceeded to Liverpool for study in Christian theology. He migrated to Canada four years after his baptism to become Professor of Hebrew and Rabbinical Literature at Bishop's University, Sherbrooke, Quebec. With the founding of Huron College, where emphasis was to be placed on "Protestant and Evangelical principles," he was appointed its first principal.⁷

"His personal magnetism was immense. He had a wonderful pair of dark brown eyes, large, mobile, luminous, keen yet kindly. One felt it was best to be thoroughly open and honest with him for then one could rely on his good will."⁸ And Isaac Barr was to need that good will over and over again when he became priest in the diocese of the newly appointed Bishop Hellmuth of Huron.

Classes were from October to the end of June, and with the beginning of the three-month holiday Barr went off to Windsor to be assistant to Canon John Hurst at All Saints'

Isaac Montgomery Barr

2227 PACIFIC AVENUE,
SPOKANE, WASH.
December
12 1901

The Reverend I. M. Barr is a Canadian Clergyman who has been officiating as rector of St. Paul's Church Whatcom, Washington. He is a man of more than usual ability a broad Churchman and alive to the issues of the day, and I commend him to the Bishops of our Communion.

Truly Yours in Christ
Lemuel H. Wells
Bishop of Spokane

Grave of Isaac Barr's mother,
Catharine Baird Barr

Letter of recommendation from the
Bishop of Spokane

MARRIAGE RETURN.

1. Date of license 25 June 1900
2. Full name of groom Isaac M. Barr
3. Age last birthday 50
4. Color (a) W.
5. No. of groom's marriages 2
6. Residence [illegible]
7. Birthplace (b) Canada
8. Occupation Clergyman
9. Father's name William Barr
10. Mother's maiden name [illegible]
11. Full name of bride Emma L. Williams

Maiden name if a widow —

12. Age last birthday 35
13. Color (a) White
14. No. of bride's marriages 0
15. Residence [illegible]
16. Birthplace (b) Ohio
17. Occupation Nurse
18. Father's name Edward Williams
19. Mother's maiden name Lydia Williams
20. Date of marriage 25 June 19[illegible]
21. Place of marriage [illegible]
22. By whom married, and official station [illegible] Clergyman
23. Names of witnesses and their residences:

No. 1 T. McElmore 562 Clark St [illegible]

No. 2 [illegible]

NOTE.—(a) State color distinctly, so race may be known, as White, Black, Mulatto, Indian, Chinese, Mixed White and Indian, etc. (b) Give state or foreign country, so nationality is plainly shown.

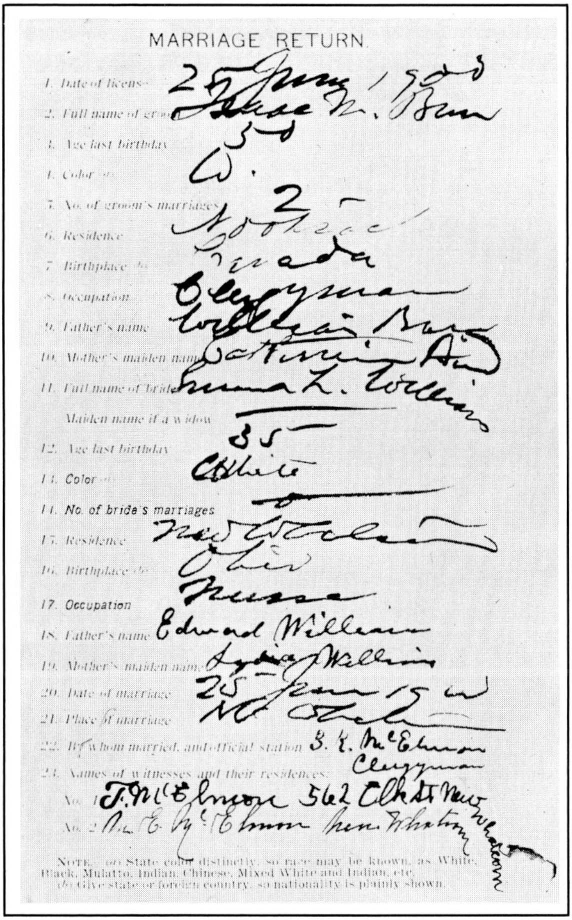

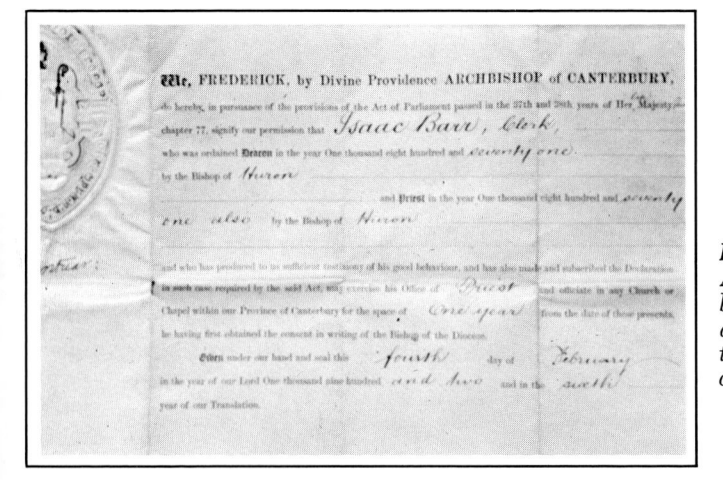

Record of marriage of Isa
Montgomery Barr and Emma
Williams: the groom's third ma
riage, the bride's first

We, FREDERICK, by Divine Providence ARCHBISHOP of CANTERBURY, do hereby, in pursuance of the provisions of the Act of Parliament passed in the 37th and 38th years of Her Majesty, chapter 77, signify our permission that Isaac Barr, Clerk, who was ordained Deacon in the year One thousand eight hundred and seventy one by the Bishop of Huron and Priest in the year One thousand eight hundred and seventy one also by the Bishop of Huron and who has produced to us sufficient testimony of his good behaviour, and has also made and subscribed the Declaration in such case required by the said Act, may exercise his Office of Priest and officiate in any Church or Chapel within our Province of Canterbury for the space of One year from the date of these presents, he having first obtained the consent in writing of the Bishop of the Diocese.

Given under our hand and seal this fourth day of February in the year of our Lord One thousand nine hundred and two and in the sixth year of our Translation.

Licence issued by t
Archbishop of Cante
bury (Frederick Temp
authorizing Isaac B
to serve as an Anglic
clergyman in Britain

Church. It was while here that he entered into the first of his several marriages.[9]

The college staff may or may not have known about this wedding. It is certain that the council took a serious view of students who married before graduation, for in 1876, six years later, it sentenced a student to "rustication [a curious word] for one year at least" for doing that very thing.[10] Other students at the college certainly knew about Barr's marriage. Evan Davis acted as best man, the bridegroom's brother, John Barr, was witness when "Isaac Barr, aged 22 of London, Ontario—parents William and Catharine Barr, and Eliza Weaver, aged 21 of Windsor, Ontario—parents John and Ann Weaver," were married August 10, 1870, by the Reverend John Hurst.[11]

The following term Barr entered the University of Toronto for an honours course in Classics and Hebrew, "but owing to my taking Holy Orders I did not proceed to a degree," he said. With apologies to the University of Toronto, this may have been considered rustication. Or perhaps he changed colleges to avoid the disciplinary action that would have been inevitable.

His bride's parents may have helped pay for the Toronto year. Isaac's relatives have always claimed that the Weavers "got him to become an Anglican by offering to pay for his education in that ministry."[12] This is possible, but unlikely. I believe Isaac was already in his second year at Huron College when he met Eliza Weaver.

For eleven dollars a month he and his wife rented a seven-room house only a short distance from the university[13, 14] and during the year Isaac's three sisters spent the winter there while they attended The Model School about two blocks away.[15]

In any event, he obtained the following standing at the University of Toronto: Classics 2; Mathematics 3 (not unexpectedly); English 2; Oriental Studies 1. He was awarded a prize in Oriental Studies.[16]

Like his father William, Isaac could certainly preach. As the words flowed forth with thundering conviction he too would be carried away by his own persuasiveness until sometimes the mere telling appeared to make it so. Swayed by his enthusiasms he often seemed more the visionary than "a young man, but of sound judgment and likely to build up the congregation" whom the deacons of Exeter requested from the bishop.[17]

To know his favourite themes would be revealing, but a study of the texts on which he preached does not disclose them.[18] He preached from short phrases or clauses that probably represent only the starting points for some soaring rhetoric.

Isaac never remained long in any one charge. In Woodstock and Exeter his problems were recurrent. The collection of his salary, modest though it was—three to four hundred dollars per year—filled the minutes of many a vestry meeting in the struggling small parishes where he preached in competition with several other denominations. Apparently his parishioners made no great effort to keep him, for in spite of his Irish background Isaac Barr lacked the light touch. He was a man with no real sense of humour[19] but, facile in debate, well read and well informed, he thrived on argument.

It must have been about this time that he began to have doubts about the doctrines of the church, though the reason he left Exeter where his first child, Dora Kathleen Barr, had been born in 1874, appears to have been indignation over the fact that the salary of four hundred dollars promised him had to be reduced to three hundred because collections were so poor.[20]

He was moving again. Recruited in Montreal by the Bishop of Saskatchewan to care for the Prince Albert Settlement in the Northwestern Territories (now Saskatchewan), he left his family in Canada and set off with a trader as far as Fort Garry. While he waited there for transportation on to Prince Albert he received a letter telling him his child was ill, but he continued his journey.

A few weeks later his bishop, travelling out to visit Barr's mission, was irritated and disappointed to meet him returning to Ontario, having abandoned his charge.[21] The bishop wrote to a colleague: "I have to inform you of a great disappointment I have had. Rev. I. Barr has resigned his position here owing to the continued illness of his wife and child whom he left in Canada. I met him on my way out. He would give no assurance of returning even next summer unless his wife's health improved, so I accepted his resignation on the spot. I unpacked my trunk on the prairie—settled accounts in writing—made him give his statement in a letter —press copied it—and that you may see what he says for himself I enclose the copy.

> Wolverine Hill
> 30 miles from Fort Ellice
> on the Prairie,
>
> 15th October 1875.

MY LORD,

It is with deep respect that I have to inform your Lordship that I have taken the serious step of leaving Prince Albert Mission without leave of your Lordship. I have not done so, it seems to me, without good reason to justify me. When I was about to leave Fort Garry for the Saskatchewan, I received a letter from my wife stating that my eldest child was dangerously ill but I felt it was my duty to go on. Since then I have heard that my wife herself is seriously ill and I [illegible] to me. Duty to the mission over which I had been placed indicated that I should remain at my post but on the other hand I felt I had a duty to discharge to my family, and after serious and I hope prayerful consideration I resolved to take upon myself the responsibility of deserting my mission and returning to Ontario to my family. I am anxious to do what is right and if your Lordship insists upon my returning this winter to do so. But I would rather not return at all than to return without my family, and as your Lordship knows that I could not bring my family out before next summer, and meanwhile the mission would be vacant. I hope that your Lordship will feel that I am anxious to do what is right and honourable and that if I have erred in leaving my mission without permission I ought to be pardoned on account of the reasons which led me to do so. I have no fault whatever to find with your Lordship—you have faithfully fulfilled every promise you made me, and it is only right that I should add that during the short period that I have laboured under your Lordship, I have found you a faithful friend and a kind Bishop, and I am sure that I could have laboured contentedly with your Lordship had my family been with me. I hope your Lordship may pardon me for deserting you and if I should not return one better fitted for the work may be found. I deeply regret that the Mission should be left vacant but I pray that it may sustain no permanent injury from any default of mine in the discharge of my duty.

With kindest wishes for your Lordship's welfare,
I remain, dear Sir your most [illegible]
ISAAC BARR[22]

It is just possible that Isaac had his tongue in his cheek when he wrote all those nice things about the bishop assuring him that he could have laboured contentedly with him had circumstances been a bit different.

On his return to Ontario Barr must have approached the Bishop of Huron, for he was assigned to a new charge in that diocese. And he was fortunate that the bishop was Hellmuth. "He always liked Dad because Dad knew Hebrew. And they had the same name, Isaac. Also Bishop Hellmuth couldn't resist trading; he always had a few diamonds in his belt. And Dad knew it."[23]

The next charge, Point Edward and Wilderness Brights Grove, lasted only two years. Barr's second child, Harry Baird Barr, was born here, July 10, 1877.[24] It is strange that in explaining his defection to the Bishop of Saskatchewan Isaac had referred to the illness of his "eldest child" unless

there was another on the way. Dora Kathleen was indeed
unwell. She suffered from epilepsy and is said by members
of the family to have had a fatal fall from her carriage.
Actually she lived into her teens.[25]

After Point Edward, Isaac was licensed to the Kanyenga
Mission on an Indian reservation near Brantford, where he
became known to the Indians by a name which meant "The
Man in the Long-tailed Coat."[26] Three years later he had
quarrelled with his employers, the New England Company,
again over money, and his engagement was terminated
with the promise that the bishop would find him yet a new
posting.

In his next parish of Teeswater, near Wingham, it took
only months until he was in trouble again. The following
letter is from Jeffrey Hill, the incumbent of a nearby parish
and rural dean, who was doing his "painful duty":

Seaforth, Ontario.

March 13, 1882.

MY LORD,

I feel that it has become my painful duty to inform your
Lordship that Mr. Barr of Wingham has, in my opinion and
that of the Deanery, given utterance to views which must
disqualify him entering a pulpit of the Church of England.
For instance, in conversation with Mr. O'Meara of Gorriem,
he deliberately pronounced the doctrine of the fall of man
"revolting" and untrue.

It is of course impossible that one holding such an opinion
can attach any real significance to the Divine Work of
Redemption, or preach the real need of a Saviour to those
the corruption of whose nature he denies.

Neither Mr. O'Meara or myself have any wish to see him
brought to trial, especially as such a course would only em-
bitter him against Christianity and mitigate against our
hopes that his conversion may yet be granted in answer to
our prayers. We trust rather that your Lordship will succeed
in inducing Mr. Barr to disclaim any desire to Bene Decessit

before the time during which a presentment can be made shall elapse, and thus obviate the necessity of open scandal or shame.

> I remain,
> Your Lordship's obdt svt,
> Jeffrey Hill[27]

Barr, however, had reacted as he was to react again and again in his life. When the going became difficult and the pressures great he backed away from a confrontation. By the time this letter reached the bishop, Barr had already resigned and gone to Winnipeg whence he wrote Bishop Hellmuth.

> Winnipeg,
>
> 8th April, 1882.

The Right Reverend,
The Lord Bishop of Huron,
Chapter House,
London, Ontario.

MY DEAR LORD BISHOP:

When I left home I had intended returning to Ontario in May when I hoped to have an interview with your Lordship and to receive my Bene Decessit. I now foresee that it may be inconvenient for me to do so or to return before next fall.

After long and prayerful consideration and after many struggles with my doubts and mental difficulties, I have come to the conclusion to act upon your Lordship's advice, not to leave the ministry, nor to cease to preach the gospel of our Saviour Christ. I have had an interview with the Bishop of Rupert's Land, who received me very kindly, and I expressed to him a desire to take duty in his diocese. He is quite willing to give me employment, but requires testimonials from my Bishop, my Rural Dean and Archdeacon. He desires to know something in regard to my moral character and ability to work a parish successfully.

I shall be greatly obliged to your Lordship if you will kindly forward to the Bishop of Rupert's Land my Bene Decessit and the testimonial he desires. I leave this country tomorrow for the Qu'Appelle district where I propose locating, and will return here in May when I hope to get my appointment. I shall hope to return to Ontario in the Autumn when I may have the opportunity of thanking your Lordship in person for all your kindness to me.

I remain, my Lord,
Your obedient Servant,
Isaac Barr.[28]

But Bishop Hellmuth had had enough. He had been lenient with Barr remembering the years of uncertainty in his own early youth. However there was no doubt that Isaac Barr "had been using the pulpit to put over his own ideas about the dogmas of the Church. He believed in the theory of evolution and preached it at a time when it was heresy to even mention it."[29]

When the bishop wrote back that, owing to the serious charges against Barr, he could not possibly issue the documents requested, all hope of employment at Qu'Appelle disappeared and Barr returned to Ontario.

By this time he had a third child, a daughter, Gertrude, and in the year following he wrote the bishop both from Point Edward and London, Ontario. Just where his family was at this time I cannot say, but by the end of the year he was prepared to ask the bishop for help, to recant, and reaffirm his beliefs in the teachings of the church. Whether the prayers of the rural dean and Mr. O'Meara had brought about this change or whether it was a matter of economic necessity, Barr wrote:

Point Edward,
19th March, 1883.

The Right Reverend,
The Lord Bishop of Huron,
Chapter House,
London.

MY LORD,

I have thought it better not to call on Mr. Hill or any of the other gentlemen who have preferred charges against me—I leave the matter entirely in your Lordship's hands believing that you will treat me with fairness and justice.

I do indeed deeply regret certain imprudent conversations with certain clergymen in which, carried away by the heat of argument, I foolishly expressed views not in harmony with the doctrines of the Church or my own real beliefs— And surely my Lord, it would be too severe a punishment to refuse me the privilege of preaching the Gospel of Xt because I have been guilty of the imprudence with which I am charged and which I now confess. I deny however that Mr. O'Meara is correct in saying that I expressed disbelief in the doctrine of the "Fall of Man." The corruption of human nature is a doctrine I fully and unequivocally accept.

Surely, my Lord, the Church does not demand more than what our Lord and Master required, namely a full and unfeigned repentance of all errors whether of the understanding or the life. I believe that God has accepted my repentance for my past life. May I not expect it then at the hands of those who rule His Church?

Hoping to hear from your Lordship after the meeting of the Standing Committee which takes place on the 29th.

I remain, My Lord,
Your obedient Servant,
Isaac Barr.[30]

In a postscript he offered "to do the work of a *Layman* in this or any other Diocese during the pleasure of the Bishop. And until he is quite satisfied that my *life* and *doctrine* are such as that I can be trusted with full clerical functions.

Life is short and I am desirous that what remains of it to me should be spent in my Master's service, nor have I any taste for other work."

Surely Isaac's real timidity led to the change. The letters show a gradual loss of bravado until finally he offers to do anything to get back in the bishop's good graces. The pressures on him—financial, family, social (a priest had real status in a community)—must have outweighed his contempt for the church's teaching and he decided henceforth to watch his words.

Three weeks later he wrote again to the bishop with what appears to be a final effort to set the matter straight. The letter reads like a full confession that "I was in error, although ever anxious to hold and teach the truth." After listing the various doctrines of the church which he accepts—the Atonement, the Trinity, the Fall of Man—he adds:

As however, a suspicion has been engendered in the public mind that I am not quite sound in doctrine it may be that my usefulness and prospects of success in your Lordship's Diocese are somewhat impaired; on this account therefore, although I shall deeply regret leaving your diocese, my Lord, I have come to the conclusion that it would be wise for me to seek work elsewhere, perhaps in some American diocese. I now ask your Lordship's permission to do so and trust that by your kind commendation, which I hope to obtain, I may be successful in finding employment in some other part of the Master's vineyard.[31]

The bishop must have felt a sense of relief: Isaac had suggested a way out. Whether his Lordship actually helped Barr to get employment in the United States I do not know. "He [Barr] always used to say he was fifty years ahead of his time, and that when he became too broad for the Canadian Church he went to the States where they were more tolerant of a man with radical ideas.[32]

Isaac Barr became rector of Grace Church, Lapeer, Michigan in 1883, and on April 16, 1885, filed papers in the district court indicating his intention of becoming an American citizen.[33] For the moment he had left off being a Canadian.

The American Years

From the records of his next diocese it appears that a sort of uneasy calm settled over the ministerial career of Isaac Barr for the next twelve years: three years at Lapeer, five years at St. Paul's, East Saginaw, one as a general missionary to the Saginaw Valley Convocation, and almost two years at St. John's Church, Midland, Michigan, from which he resigned in 1893. The next two years are lost, for he was noted twice as "absent from convention," suggesting that since he was expected he was still in the area.[1] Where?

He had remained five years at St. Paul's, longer than he had stayed in any one parish or ever would. But from then on he appears to have become restless again. Perhaps the Americans were not as "broad" as he had at first judged them to be. Or it may have been that his domestic life had by this time become so entangled and uncertain that it again seemed better to shift the site of his labours to "some other part of the Master's vineyard."

His family was with him in Michigan and descendants say that during this time his wife conducted tours to Rome and other parts of Italy. Perhaps this is true. They also say that this first marriage ended in an American divorce; that his wife "ran off with a wealthy man, a doctor, and they lived in Italy" and since Isaac was the aggrieved party he could still continue as a clergyman in the Episcopal Church.[2] (If this is true it might account for his lifetime contempt for all doctors.) His intention to become an American citizen may have been related to the divorce, though from the dates involved it appears unlikely. Intensive search has failed to locate a record of this divorce petition but it is certain that it did not take place in Canada.[3] Perhaps his descendants are mistaken, for fifteen years after he filed his intent to become an American citizen, his wife was still known as Mrs. Eliza T. Barr.[4]

Isaac's next appearance on the religious scene, after the two "lost" years, was in the mountains of Tennessee in 1896, at Harriman, where he delighted his bishop with his zeal and impressed him with his success as a missionary. Bishop Quintard so liked Barr's preaching that he appointed him to a committee to compose a fitting Memorial Statement on the death of a distinguished Tennessee divine.[5] The following notes appear in the bishop's diary:

April 25, 1897. At eleven o'clock services were held in the village school house. The missionary, the Reverend Isaac M. Barr, said Morning Prayer. I preached, confirmed twenty-four candidates and addressed them. . . . The services were closed by a marriage at which Mr. Barr officiated. Accompanied by Mr. Barr I left Glen Mary (112 miles north from Chattanooga) at 3.30 for Harriman where I arrived at 5 p.m. At night Mr. Barr said evening prayer and I preached. I wish to call special attention to the faithful missionary work of the Rev. Isaac Barr. Before Morning Prayer I visited the Sunday School where I found no less than 150 pupils. The class for confirmation presented by Mr. Barr was the largest confirmed by me in any parish or mission in the last year. Mr. Barr has an immense field and is doing a wonderful work. He is endeavouring to build a church in Glen Mary. I pray God he may succeed. He should be encouraged by the Clergy and the churchmen throughout the Diocese.[6]

November 22, 1898. I went to Glen Mary . . . the work here is progressing well and the new chapel, a most substantial and churchly structure, will be ready for occupancy by Christmas. Mr. Barr deserves to be congratulated on having brought the mission up to such a satisfactory condition.[7]

The bishop liked him and so did the mountaineers. He had become a friend, and while he ranted against the evils of drink from the pulpit he was sympathetic to his parishioners. The fact that on occasion he "would take a little" himself may have accounted for his high conversion rate. It certainly endeared him to them. As he went about his mission field and visited with them in their little cabins the talk naturally drifted to moonshine, and when they found that he was neither revenuer nor informer the talk could become explicit and even boastful. They trusted him—well, almost. Finally, they agreed to show him.

One warm night in the bright of the moon he joined a small party of moonshiners. They blindfolded him and then led him on horseback into the hills. He sensed that the route was circuitous and at times felt certain they doubled back on their tracks. In any case he was hopelessly lost. Suddenly the horses broke into a little clearing. As the blindfold was removed he dimly made out a crude shed of weathered boards sheltered under an overhang of rock. From cob to crock they showed him how it was done. Together they sampled the stock and sampled it again, and as the early light fingered the mountain tops the blindfold was replaced and the party rode for home. The route was less devious this time. Perhaps the mountaineers were a little careless by now or they were willing to rely on the effect of the night's imbibitions. In the full light of the morning they were not so sure; the next day the preacher received a letter threatening his life if ever he informed on them.[8]

It was a few weeks later that Isaac had his first chill. For days he lay in a state of near-coma with malaria, as cycle followed cycle. When the bouts of fever gradually subsided he realized that it was the coloured nurse tending him constantly as he fought for survival who had saved his life. Though the attacks became weaker and farther apart he suffered from malaria until he was an old, old man.[9]

In spite of his bishop's high praise, by the fall of 1899, just months after Barr's chapel in Glen Mary was complete, another priest had taken over the mission, and the diocesan office can find no mention of the bishop issuing a dismissory letter for Mr. Barr.[10] Had they quarrelled? Was Isaac retreating from yet another confrontation? Were his marital affairs so involved that he had to move on?

From Tennessee, Isaac went to New Whatcom, Washington. On October twentieth his son Harry Baird Barr, by now twenty-two years old, had joined the army in Toronto for service in the Boer War, giving his father in Washington as his next of kin. Six months later Harry was dead of dysentery at Naauwpoort, South Africa, but it was his mother, still listed as Mrs. Eliza Barr as late as November of 1901, living in Windsor, Ontario, who signed for his medals.[11] Perhaps after all she never married her wealthy doctor.

On June 25, 1900, Isaac Barr entered into another marriage, apparently his third, this one in New Whatcom.[12] The document of licence seems only to confuse rather than clarify the picture of his marriages. The bride was a nurse, Emma L. Williams of New Whatcom, and Isaac stated that he had not one but two previous marriages! On that part of the original record relative to the bride, *Item 13: Colour,* what appears to have been a *C* is overwritten to form a *W* and continued to read "White." Had the writer started the word "Caucasian" or could Emma Williams have been the "coloured" nurse who saved his life in the Tennessee Mountains just the year before? One of the witnesses to this ceremony is still alive but so frail that he cannot recall the details, and though I sought intensively in Ohio for the bride's birth record I found no positive proof of birth or colour.

What became of Emma Williams Barr, whether she died or whether she and Isaac were divorced, is lost. She had no registered offspring in Washington up to a year after her husband had left. Neither her death nor divorce are recorded in England, where Isaac went, nor in Canada nor in Ohio, her home state, nor yet in Tennessee where it is possible that she met Isaac. It is not recorded in Dakota, the residence given by Isaac when he entered into his fourth marriage, nor in Nebraska, the state in which the fourth marriage took place.

And what of the second Mrs. Barr, the lady whose marriage is revealed simply by the statement on the application for licence, *No. of groom's marriages. 2?* Perhaps she belongs to the two lost American years or the time in Tennessee. I could find no further trace of her.

All this time Isaac continued as an Anglican priest. The third marriage took place openly in his own parish and he frankly admitted to the two previous ones. The first Mrs. Barr was still living, giving credence to the story that Isaac had been the aggrieved party in a divorce action and hence could continue to serve in the church. There is still another tradition. Some members of the family, when talking of the end of the first marriage, have said, "He ran off with another woman."[13] It would be hard to know what the truth is. However, the daughter of the first marriage, Gertrude, corresponded with her father and his family years after he was married for the fourth time and had left the county. Had she believed her own mother to be a discarded wife she would scarcely have kept up this link.

But about one thing there can be little doubt. Isaac was attractive to women: "He was a soft-spoken courteous man when you met him. Fine-looking too. You could not help but trust him. But you didn't exactly warm to him. But then I'm not a woman."[14]

As the century approached its close the talk was all of empire, the British Empire. In the press and from the platform the imperialists waved the flag. The aging Victoria had been crowned Empress of India; the North American Colonies, the Canadas and the Maritimes were now part of a dominion to which British Columbia on the far-off Pacific coast had just been added. And Rhodes, in Africa, seemed about to extend the chain of empire from Cape to Cairo.

For several years Germany, Portugal, Belgium and England struggled for resource-rich Africa, each striving by negotiation with native tribal leaders, by purchase and political manoeuvre to acquire rights to the land. Rhodes used all these means.

He was a man who saw his schemes not just as dreams but as plans. He knew that to hold a land it must be occupied and so by 1890 he had begun the business of recruiting, organizing, equipping and routing a company of pioneers, "fit and preferably unmarried; men who were first-class shots, and if possible had experience of, or an aptitude for, some trade; in fact they were to be a community in embryo."

After some sifting a likely lot of pioneers had been enrolled. They included farmers, artisans, miners, doctors, lawyers, engineers, builders, bakers, soldiers, sailors, cadets of good family and no special occupation (an interesting qualification), cricketers, three parsons and a Jesuit.

"There were two hundred pioneers, five hundred mounted police and a large contingent of native porters"— about a thousand in all—who set out for Mount Hampden to occupy and hold the territory that was to become Rhodesia.[15]

Newspapers all over the world carried the story of the pioneers. As Barr read all this and more he began to identify himself with Rhodes.

"I walked between earth and sky and when I looked down I said, 'This earth shall be English,' and when I looked up I said, 'The English should rule this earth.' A world dominated by the British would be a better place; and the kind of life the British brought with them, representing the distilled wisdom of the ages, the best that was in Greece and Rome and the Christian Ethic, was worthier than any other kind."[16] Rhodes was saying it, the British politicians were saying it.

Isaac pored over the reports and in his dreaming he saw himself another Rhodes. They were contemporaries. Both were children of the manse; both had a stepmother. Rhodes spoke of spending long hours as a youth with a retired admiral of eighty years who lived nearby, and Barr had spent hours with Captain John Baird. Neither went to a

regular school. Rhodes was educated at a small local grammar school with a view to going into the ministry; Barr was
educated at home and in a local private school and did enter
that profession. Both might be said to have been "of no fixed
address," for they wandered widely and restlessly in a time
of limited travel. Rhodes had his emigration scheme and
Barr was to have his. But here the likeness ends. Barr was no
Rhodes. Impractical, trusting, poor, Barr should have been
warned by the problems that Rhodes met and overcame.
They had all been chronicled in the papers of the times. His
problems with the British government, the committees that
enquired into his affairs and into the results of his colonization schemes were news.

Rhodes' colonists had real problems.

He ... paid his first visit to his territory just over a year after
the arrival of the pioneers. Plenty of troubles were waiting
for him. Every river had overflowed its banks and the whole
country was under water. The settlers were cut off from one
another and from their supplies. Many actually died of
starvation or fever; and the survivors, being without cattle
or crops, were reduced to living on pumpkins and millet
brought from the nearest kraal. Many were so discouraged
that they returned to the south though these were mostly
those who had swarmed into the country in the wake of the
pioneers hoping for easy gold.
The land was infested by lions, but almost more trouble-
some were the rats which descended on the settlements,
devouring any stores they could reach and even nibbling
the fingers and toes of the sleepers. One audacious rat even
made off with Jameson's false teeth, which were lying in a
tumbler of water by his bedside. After the rats came the
snakes, some of them extremely poisonous. Even to a settled
community, the winter would have been a sore trial; to the
pioneers it was a disaster. In their extremity they were in-
clined to lay the blame of their misfortune on the Chartered
Company [that is, Rhodes].

Rhodes' colonists had real grievances too. Every pioneer
had been promised three hundred acres of freehold but
the land was not the company's to give away. The man

who had come north hoping for a gold mine and expecting at any rate a farm began to believe he would get neither. Worst of all was the complete lack of communications. Even when the rains ended and the road was open again, haulage from the railhead cost from three hundred to three hundred and fifty dollars per ton; and the settlers were still having to import everything they needed. Rhodes did what he could to hasten the extension of the railway and telegraph from the south, but the work was slow and the need was desperate.[17]

The parallel does not end here.

To ensure his personal immortality, Rhodes, who dying asked to be reassurred again and again that the name Rhodesia would survive, had had his own colony scheme. Barr was to have his: a trek by a selected band of colonists, far beyond the railroad lines, to establish a frontier community of good British stock that would hold Canada to the British Empire, and would, just incidentally, be called Barrview. In the dream, the purpose, the journey, the hardship, the dissatisfaction and even the committee of enquiry of the British parliament, Barr was to be the pale copy of Rhodes.

Late in December, 1901, eighteen months after his third marriage, Isaac announced that he was resigning from his charge and leaving for South Africa to enter into a settlement scheme with Cecil Rhodes. His vestrymen thought highly of their minister; they expressed regret at his departure and commended him to churchmen everywhere but particularly in South Africa.

For an imperialist like Barr the Boer War was a just war. South Africa should belong to the empire; his own son had fought and died to achieve this. But not all Americans agreed with him. There had been considerable pro-Boer sympathy in the State of Washington. The Americans had thrown off British domination and they would be happy to see their success repeated.

Isaac undertook to dissuade them from this view. He organized the British-American Club at Whatcom. Since the membership consisted largely of those of British descent and sympathetic Americans, its influence was probably of little significance, except that it brought the embryo empire builder to the attention of Bernard Pelly, the British Vice-Consul at Seattle, who, in a letter dated December 10, 1901, wrote:

> I have learned that you have resigned the rectorship of St. Paul's Church and intend to go to South Africa. I am sorry that you will have to sever your connection with the British-American Club at Whatcom. As its president you have been able to take a leading part in bringing Britishers and Americans into closer sympathy and endeavouring to make some of the rough places smooth. You have probably realized as I have done that most of the pro-Boer agitation in these parts has been for political purposes, and I know that the bringing together of those of British descent and those in sympathy with the objects of our club has done much to promote good fellowship. I fully recognize that when your club was started the position you took was unpopular and the task a thankless one and I wish that you were going to remain and carry on the good work until after the final settlement of our trouble in South Africa....[18]

The colonization scheme with Cecil Rhodes was probably never more than a dream in the mind of Isaac Barr. Time was against him. Rhodes was only briefly in England in January, 1902, and was, even at that time, a dying man hard-pressed by his own problems with the British government. He died March 26, 1902, in Capetown.

A search of the Rhodes memorabilia in the library at Salisbury revealed no correspondence on the subject of a joint venture and no mention of Isaac Barr.[19] The curator of the Rhodes Library at Oxford, where the bulk of the Rhodes Papers are kept, is definite: there is no record of any contact between the two men, though some of the papers relative to this period were lost in the bombing of Britain.[20]

But Barr had started to build the empire. The death of Queen Victoria in January, 1901, moved him to pay public tribute to Her Majesty in a message which not only revealed the depth of his British ties but presented a fair sampling of his style.

From the *Daily Reveille*, New Whatcom, February 5, 1901:

A QUEENLY MEMORIAL

.... To those who have heard him before, Mr. Barr needs no introduction as a speaker. His remarks were forceful and eloquent, and portrayed the late queen as she was. He pictured her as a woman to whom birth had bequeathed greatness, but whom womanly qualities had made noble and pure. As a queen she was loved and respected by her own people, but as a woman she was loved and respected by all people and in every home. He pictured the deathbed and showed that though at death's door her thoughts were for those who had watched by her bedside to administer to her comfort. He emphasized the solemnity of the death chamber and the effect it had had upon all nations, especially to [sic] the Anglo-Saxon.

The speaker went on to show the effect the life of Queen Victoria has had upon the present generation and will have upon the generations to come. As a woman, her womanly qualities will be a guiding star to nobler, purer womanhood and higher and grander virtues, and as a queen a glorious example of "peace on earth goodwill toward all men."[21]

Barr got only as far as England on his imperialistic journey. He likely reached London the end of January, 1902. Any hope he had of a colonization scheme in South Africa had now vanished. On February fourth the Archbishop of Canterbury licensed him to preach in England,[22] so Isaac remained in London and began a ministry as a holiday replacement for the curate-in-charge of St. Saviour's Church, Tollington Park, London, N.[23]

But for Barr the pattern was set. His dedication to the empire, initiated fifty years before in the tales of Catharine Barr, reinforced by the Bairds, nurtured by his own identification with the Rhodes' legend, was about to become transformed into The Barr Colony. For the time being he had left off being an American.

Panoply of Empire

It was the year of empire—1902. The Boer War was drawing to a close and the response of the "daughter states" had swelled the tide of emotional attachment between Britain and her colonies. "The zeal for the progress of the Empire and an appreciation of its benefits . . . is a phenomenon which has come so suddenly . . . in so vast a volume . . . that it indicated an amount of feeling which we did not here realize, which under the stress of circumstances and under the impulse of a strong sympathy has made itself felt throughout the Empire. We have no power to affect the flow of opinion and affection which has arisen so largely between the Mother country and her daughter states. They will go on in their power, in their irresistible power, and, I have no doubt they will leave combinations behind them which will cast into shade all the glories that the British Empire has hitherto displayed," said Lord Salisbury.[1]

"Call us to your councils!" pleaded Sir Wilfrid Laurier, the Canadian Prime Minister, who was pushing for a legislated Union of Empire; and further to spread the pan-Britannic gospel, Joseph Chamberlain added, "We must draw closer our internal relations, the ties of sentiment, the ties of sympathy, yes the ties of interest."[2]

England and the empire had just won a war. The influential *Fortnightly Review* of the time said:

In the last resource it is on sentiment, on the passionate, well-nigh religious attachment of British subjects to Eng-

42

land and the British Crown, on their pride of race and of communion in a great past that the Empire rests . . . men and women born in the colonies, never having seen England and with little expectation of seeing it . . . thought and spoke of it as "home" and "the old country" . . . This gives us a glimpse of the silken thread that makes the Empire one.[3]

As the certain periodical test of the quality of a nation, no substitute for war has been discovered. It is in itself an immense stimulus and usually raises creative energy to a higher power in a way that does far more than merely repair in a short time the waste of life and wealth it causes. A decade ago . . . it was the opinion of many of us that nothing would be so good for England as a just war that would rouse her to the core. We have had our struggle . . . conditions have been perhaps the least favourable to a good moral effect . . . But it has not given us the inspiration that we should have derived from a really great war against another first class power, with our existence at stake. . . .[4]

Perhaps this war in South Africa had not been the perfect one. But in order to hold the territorial gains she had made, Britain had decided, on the advice of Cecil Rhodes and that of a commissioner sent to South Africa to determine how this could best be done, that it would require fifteen thousand Englishmen scattered as settlers among the Boers to hold the land for the Empire.[5]

It had not been the perfect war at home either. As the waves of returning soldiers, many of them in broken health, reached London to face hardship and unemployment, Isaac, as a clergyman, came to know some of them well, to realize their hopelessness and frustration and to pity their uncertainty. "There was a miserable, dreary, grinding drudgery for the working man. He had to wait for a dead man's shoes after he finished his apprenticeship, for there was no future for him. There was much unfairness in labour practices and there were no labour unions to improve his lot."[6]

By April of 1902 the country as a whole was enjoying a great surge of patriotism. There had been victory at arms, the coronation of Edward VII, planned for June twenty-sixth, was imminent, and the erection of viewing stands and special displays was well advanced. Visiting royalty and heads of state arrived almost daily for the celebrations. State functions, parades, martial music, pomp and circumstance, it was all British and it was all empire!

Then suddenly, three days before the appointed ceremony, the King fell ill and, remarkably for those times, survived the removal of his appendix. Though the celebrations were halted temporarily, the sentiment remained, centred on the person of Edward. As he continued to improve, the excitement was on again, heightened by the press and the daily bulletins. Six weeks later he was crowned in Westminster Abbey.

It had been a royal summer of flags, bunting and burning patriotism; of imperialistic dreams and national glory; of speech making and processions. Isaac was ready and he had become filled; filled with a kind of glory, an imperial zeal that would touch him with greatness and ultimately destroy him. For the moment he had found his place in history.

But now Barr's interest had switched from holding South Africa to filling up the empty spaces of the Canadian Northwest by settling them with people truly British. He knew the country west of Winnipeg, the Qu'Appelle and Prince Albert districts. He had driven over the prairies in between, in what is now Saskatchewan. And he was well aware that American and European immigrants were rushing into the area for the free-grant land offered by the Canadian government.

Two weeks after the coronation he began his campaign, bombarding the newspapers with letters to the editors, giving interviews to the press and speaking in public wherever and whenever he could arrange it. He described the richness of the land and how it could be farmed; there were no trees to be cut, roots to be grubbed or rocks to be blasted out. It would be easy clearing.

In his speeches and in his writings to the press Isaac offered two things: an exchange of the poverty of Britain for an estate in Canada; a chance to build the empire by

planting a colony of pure British culture in the empty territory.[7] The offer was irresistible.

Another Canadian clergyman, resident in London, the
Reverend George Exton Lloyd, wrote enthusiastic letters to
the newspapers at this same time, telling of that land of
opportunity, the Canadian West, and saying that it should
be settled by British people.[8] Among the hundreds of replies
he received was a letter from Isaac Barr requesting an
interview and stating that he was trying to arrange a colonization scheme in the same area. The two men met and
decided to work together, Lloyd turning over all his enquiries to Barr. The extent of Lloyd's co-operation at this
time is not stated in his memoirs, beyond the fact that from
time to time he dropped in at the offices Barr had set up to
handle the organization of the plan.[9]

In late September Barr issued his first pamphlet under the
title *British Settlement in North Western Canada on Free
Grant Lands—Canada for the British!*[10] It opened with the
quotation: "And so more and more I can't help looking to
the west. There is the world as the world will be. There are
the things one hopes for, and cares for and lives for."* The
pamphlet continued:

THE PROJECT

To organize a large body of British people of the right kind—
English, Scotch and Irish—to form a settlement on government free grant lands, on the prairies of North-west Canada.

ADVANTAGES OF A PARTY

Companionship, mutual help and encouragement, the absence of isolation and loneliness, organized protection of
interests, larger and more rapidly increasing land values,
better railway facilities, better roads, better and cheaper
goods, schools, churches, stores, purchase at greatly reduced
prices of farm stock and implements as well as building
material for houses, furniture and provisions, all and much
more, the immediate front of a large British settlement co-
operating under proper leadership to secure the best results.

---

*John Richard Green, *A Short History of the English People* (London:
1874).

Under categories wanted, he listed "experienced farmers and their sons, artisans, tradesmen, some professional men, young men who desire to learn farming and farm labourers." He announced that he was charging no fees for his services but did request return postage.

THE LEADER OF THE MOVEMENT is a self-description: "I was born on a large farm in Canada and learned all branches of agriculture. With me farming has always been an enthusiasm, and I might also say a passion, and I have farmed both in Canada and the United States." He included the doubtful statement, "I have done some fairly good work as a colonizer," and continued, "I am now anxious to build up my native land and keep it as much as possible in the hands of people of British birth." He closed his account of "The Leader" by saying he did not intend to be the clergyman of the settlement.

Clearly stating that this would be no communistic settlement, he went on to discuss the date of departure from Britain. The trip was to be a bargain. There would be no charge for luggage and he especially mentioned "musical instruments," without distinguishing between piccolo or piano, trumpet or tuba.

He wrote of the heavy clothing and household goods needed and described the colonist cars:

The journey inland to the Northwest will be over the Canadian Pacific Railway in colonist and tourist cars, which afford comfortable sleeping accommodation. In these cars there is absolute privacy and objectionable persons are strictly excluded. There is a porter in every car to look after the comfort of the passengers. Each car is provided with a range on which passengers may, without charge, cook food, make tea, coffee, etc. Food, either cooked or uncooked, may be bought very cheaply at all stations on the road. Single persons would no doubt buy their food at stations but families can save money by using their own food on the cars. Those who contemplate doing so should take baskets, knives, forks, spoons, tinplates, drinking cups.

Then followed a long description of how to obtain free-grant land; how to obtain additional land; a note on planting and plowing; the probable cost of housing; a plan for a training home farm for "Inexperienced Young Men of Considerable Means"; bank borrowing. He closed with a statement of the social advantages of the settlement in a positive tone which, while it suggested the problems and difficulties they would face, ended:

I do not desire to present a picture that is highly rose coloured. There are difficulties and drawbacks to be encountered; but for the brave man obstacles are something to be overcome and stepping stones to victory and success. Britons have ever been the great colonizers; let it not be said that we are the degenerate sons of brave and masterful sires. . . .

Barr continued:

HARD WORK BEFORE EVERYONE

Let me say in brief you cannot pick up nuggets of gold on the surface of the soil; you must dig for the wealth of the land. Hard work and plenty of it lies before you, more or less of hardship and not seldom privations. You must sweat, and sometimes suffer from the cold. You shall not always find everything to your hand. Many of the comforts of England you must leave behind.

Some of the crops may not be a perfect success, many may even prove a failure. It may even be that hail may sometimes strike your crop and destroy part of it. Sickness may come to you there as here, and also loss. Don't expect to be rich in a day. It is not possible anywhere, except for a few fortunate ones.

If you are afraid, stay at home—don't come to Canada. It is a land of brave and conquering men. But if you are honest and brave and intend to work hard, if you propose to lead the temperate and strenuous life, then come and cast your lot with us and we will stand together and win.

The Canadian government wanted these people. Sir Wilfrid Laurier, the Prime Minister, and Clifford Sifton, his

Minister of the Interior, pressed for new settlers for the western territories and made it clear that they preferred people from the British Isles. The Canadian Pacific Railway wanted them too. Someone had to provide the market for the thousands of sections of land the company had been given by the government as an inducement to build. The rush was on. Immigrants were arriving by the shipload from all the European countries: Germany, Poland and the Ukraine—all land hungry. From across the border the Americans flooded in, not only as homesteaders but as land speculators, buying up all the property they could get, especially along the projected railway lines.

So great was the pressure that the Canadian government would not undertake to reserve the land for the colony beyond April 15, 1903, a scant six months away, by which time the members had to be on the land.

Time was short and lessening. There was a sense of urgency and excitement about the whole movement. It was the hour for decision and action. Spurred on by the two clerics, almost two thousand people signed up for a migration originally intended for about five hundred.

On the thirtieth of September, 1902, Barr himself sailed for Canada to select the exact site of the reservation and to make the arrangements necessary for the transport and location of the colony.[11] Pamphlet Number Two, dated Christmas, 1902,[12] details his plans for the colony on the basis of what he had been able to arrange. The accomplishment is staggering in view of the short time available, the transportation difficulties and the indifferent communications systems in the new land.

It is in this document that he revealed for the first time that trusting naivety, that dependence on the word of other people that was to contribute so much to his personal tragedy. Impressed by officialdom, he appears to have taken the word of almost everyone, expecting them to live up to their commitments, where a tougher, more experienced man would have known that in the vast unorganized territory, so delicate a timetable would be impossible to keep, that the sudden enormous needs of so large a group would impose demands that could not be met, no matter how willing the guarantor.

The new document was detailed and specific:

From Mr. Hanna [third vice-president of the Canadian Northern Railway] I received the assurance that the C.N.R. would be completed through to Edmonton by 1903, and would traverse the entire length of the townships I had in view. He also, after consulting Mr. William MacKenzie [*sic*], the President of the Railway, gave me a pledge that railway construction would be begun through our settlement soon after my party arrived, and that members of the party needing to earn wages, would be put to work on the roadbed at a wage per diem which would be very generous. With this assurance I felt I was proceeding on a solid and satisfactory basis.

They had shown Barr the maps of the proposed line and he had no reason to doubt the forecasts: "It will be ready to haul out the harvest of 1903." The trusting dreamer!

The soil was rich, he went on, the water plentiful; by sinking wells eight to twenty feet a good flow was certain. He had arranged for timber for building to be floated as rafts down the Saskatchewan River from Edmonton. There was wood for fuel and coal would be available when the railroad came through "a few months after we reach the location."

He brought back to London samples of wheat, other grains and vegetables grown in the area; wheat, twenty-five to fifty bushels per acre, and flax, eighteen to twenty-four bushels per acre and selling at a dollar per bushel. He told of the rich pasturage, the grasses yielding twenty-four tons per acre; the small wild fruits, the fish and the game. And all he said was true.

To the prairie-born his description of the climate is no exaggeration: the high, clear prairie sky and the brilliant lemon sunshine, winter and summer. But he made the mistake of quoting the *Saskatchewan Herald* (Battleford): "In climate the district is highly favourable, blizzards, cyclones and tornadoes being unknown [true—except for the blizzards] and extremes of heat and cold are of rare occurrence [perhaps thirty below is not extreme]."

For those who chose to work a year before settling, wages were $1.20 to $2.00 per day and from twenty dollars a month, board included.

The homestead regulations were clearly stated. "Every male over 18 is entitled to a homestead or free grant of 160 acres—a quarter of a section. Every woman too, who is the sole head of a family, can enter for a homestead. The entry fee is $10.00. The homesteader must perfect his entry by beginning actual residence on his homestead within six months of making entry." (Within limits this period could be extended by special permission from the Minister of the Interior.) The six months of residency per year, for each of the three consecutive years, necessary to get title, need not be consecutive months. This permitted homesteaders to leave their land for seasonal work elsewhere, without endangering their ownership. The government made no stipulation regarding the value of the house to be erected on the site.

Barr informed his colonists that he had made arrangements with the Elder Dempster (Beaver Line) Company for a ship which would be specially refitted to meet their requirements. Fares were forty dollars per adult, cabin class, with children under twelve half-fare, and under one year, free; for third class about $27.50 with the same consideration for children. There was no charge for excess baggage, "if it is not much beyond the quantity allowed. Small dogs such as fox terriers will be taken free, but large dogs must be paid for." He had even arranged for a bill of fare to be mailed to each prospective passenger.

The colonists were to step from ship to train at Saint John, New Brunswick. The rate from there to the railhead at Saskatoon was $22.50 by colonist car for adults, with special consideration for children, the under-fives travelling free. He had also arranged, he thought, for tourist cars for women and children if they wished to transfer to them from the colonist cars, but "it would be impossible to provide tourist cars for all; and indeed single men should be prepared to rough it a little. It is better to begin at once."

Barr described both types of accommodation clearly and accurately and listed what would be needed for the journey in the unupholstered colonist cars: "pillows, blankets (a good supply), drop curtains with safety pins to fasten them to be suspended in front of the berths, soap and towels." Straw mattresses could be rented from the railway at the point of debarkation.

He explained fully about food being available at the stopping points but again he foolishly trusted the CPR to be sure there was sufficient for a party this size, though he warned his colonists to take provisions with them.

In telling the story of Barr it is necessary to dwell on the things outlined in the pamphlet, for in the months to come the settlers were to claim that they had been misinformed and misled by Isaac Barr, and to turn against him because he had misrepresented the West to them.

In his description of Saskatoon, the railhead, he warned them it was only a village of a few hundred, informed them of the number and variety of stores and services and made it clear that here they would have to live in tents as there were no hotels. He told them he would arrange for the transportation of women and children to the colony site, but they would have to be prepared to pay for this service. In fact, he recommended that women and children be left at home, to follow later in, say, six months if they were not sturdy. In any case he recommended that they should not go unless they had "sufficient means," whatever that might be.

He did not promise them schools would be waiting but outlined how they could be financed and how the colony could organize itself to have a government-supported school. He wanted a library too and made arrangements for the free transport of donated books to start one.

Outlining the businesses that would be possible in the community he said, "I would like to hear at once from men of capital who would be willing to engage in business other than farming," and called a meeting of them in his office for January 12, 1903, suggesting that they might plan to go out in advance of the party to make the necessary purchases.

In a section entitled OUR NEIGHBOURS WHEN WE REACH THE SETTLEMENT he said, "From Saskatoon to the townships reserved we shall pass through a lovely country that is rapidly being settled. Thousands beside ourselves will land at Saskatoon next spring and go west along the same trail to lands adjoining our own on all sides." With a nod for the Europeans, Americans and "Scotch servants of the Hudson's Bay Company and their descendants, with a slight mixture of Indian blood, which only makes them the more interesting," he went on to reassure prospective settlers about the Indians:

All Indians in the Northwest Canada are now practically civilized. They live on reservations, in houses of their own building, and farm the soil under government instructors, possessing in many cases, fine herds of cattle and horses. There are some reservations about 30 or 40 miles from our settlement, and I met many of their people and conversed with them. They are now quiet and law-abiding citizens. There are only about 20,000 scattered over the whole vast Northwest. There is nothing to fear from our Indian friends any more than from the gypsies of England.

As the time for departure neared Isaac became more and more involved. He had set up a larger office at 14 Serjeants' Inn and had hired Mr. George Flamank as secretary and Christina Helberg, an attractive London-born clerk-typist. Christina was young, and as she typed the words that flowed each day from the pen of Isaac Barr she too became caught up with the enthusiasm of the man, and was carried away by his vision and sense of mission. While he had been in Canada, Lloyd had taken over for him, and when Barr returned to England Lloyd continued at the office conducting most of the personal interviews, and answering queries. "Yes, if you are healthy, go, go, go west. If you are strong, go west. If you have a hundred pounds then go west!"[13] Lloyd urged one colonist. Meanwhile Barr and his small staff were preoccupied with the logistics of the colony scheme.

Lloyd wrote:

[I was] really surprised at the number of letters that came to me asking about the religious side of life out there: would there be any church? About services? And what would the children do about Sunday school? I could only write back what little I knew about the district from the church year-book, and that was not very much when it came to answering definite questions. There was a clergyman in Battleford . . . but that was a hundred miles from where they were going to settle, besides he was the Mounted Police chaplain and could not be away very often, but I felt sure he would do all he could to help.

All this was very indefinite and I felt it to be very unsatisfactory. So I put all these letters on the table at the Colonial and Continental Church Society . . .

The committee ultimately agreed to support a chaplain to the colony for three years, and advertised in the church papers for a clergyman to go out with the party but stipulated that he must have some Canadian experience. . . . The Society not having found a clergyman with Canadian experience the matter came squarely back to me—it was I or nothing. I went home to consult my wife and she thought it would be wrong to let a large party (as it was evidently going to be) go out without a clergyman, and so, five weeks before the party sailed, we sold up what little we had gathered together of household things, and with five small children, were in Liverpool ready to sail on the SS *Lake Manitoba*.[14]

The frenzy of the pace went on. Barr had arranged ship charter; special trains in detail down to local ticketing; he had collected figures on crop prospects in the new land. He knew the prices of horses, cows, plows, mowers, binders, hayrakes, axes, wagons, lumber by the foot, windows, shingles; he had arranged for stock to be at the railhead when the colonists arrived, tents for their temporary housing, and blankets for the trip. He had purchased five hundred Russian stoves to be on the site at Saskatoon, and had arranged even such details as the money-changers who would come aboard the ship at Saint John to change English currency to Canadian dollars before the party disembarked. Almost daily he fired off a steady stream of directives to the prospective colonists informing them of details and reminding them often that this was really a scheme for people of some means.

All this had been accomplished by Barr, miraculously, with almost no money. His small personal funds were spent in printing the first pamphlet. He received commissions from the steamship company which went to pay rent and clerk hire. The CPR and the Beaver Line financed his trip to Canada to select the colony site and made him an agent for the sale of CPR lands adjoining the homesteads. He had hopes that the Canadian government would pay him a capitation fee when he landed his party in the territory reserved for him, but this he never received.[15]

Realizing that he alone could not finance stores and provisioning on anything like the necessary scale, nor could the local merchants in Saskatoon provide sufficient stocks even though they were warned in advance of the coming of a party so large, he undertook the first of his syndicates. Whether this was the result of the meeting of those "men of capital interested in going into business" in the colony or because of reluctance on their part to enter into small individual businesses I do not know. THE BRITISH CANADIAN SETTLEMENT STORES SYNDICATE IN THE SASKATCHEWAN VALLEY was a corporation on a grand scale for the purpose of supplying the settlers with groceries, provisions, clothing, drapery, ironmongery, furniture, implements, farm and garden seeds, wagons, horses, cattle and so forth. It was a splendid idea for making the settlement self-contained and self-supporting, for the profits would stay within the group; but it proved also to be a splendid idea for rousing the local merchants in Saskatoon and Battleford against the colony. The business provided by this huge block of settlers would

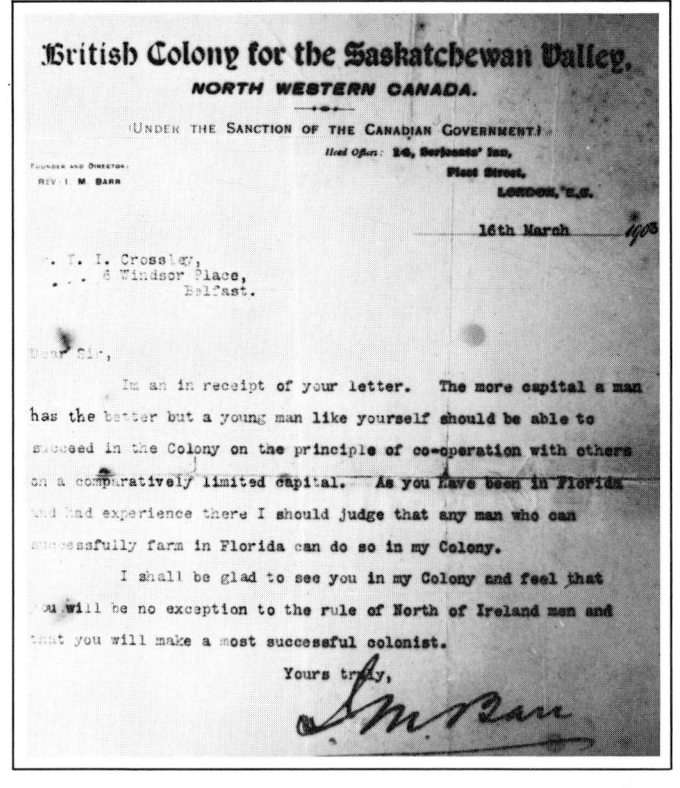

British Colony for the Saskatchewan Valley,

NORTH WESTERN CANADA.

(UNDER THE SANCTION OF THE CANADIAN GOVERNMENT.)

Founder and Director:
REV. I. M. BARR

Head Office: 16, Serjeants' Inn,
Fleet Street,
LONDON, E.C.

16th March 1903

. T. I. Crossley,
6 Windsor Place,
Belfast.

Dear Sir,

Im an in receipt of your letter. The more capital a man has the better but a young man like yourself should be able to succeed in the Colony on the principle of co-operation with others on a comparatively limited capital. As you have been in Florida and had experience there I should judge that any man who can successfully farm in Florida can do so in my Colony.

I shall be glad to see you in my Colony and feel that you will be no exception to the rule of North of Ireland men and that you will make a most successful colonist.

Yours truly,

I. M. Barr

tter from Isaac Barr
a prospective colonist

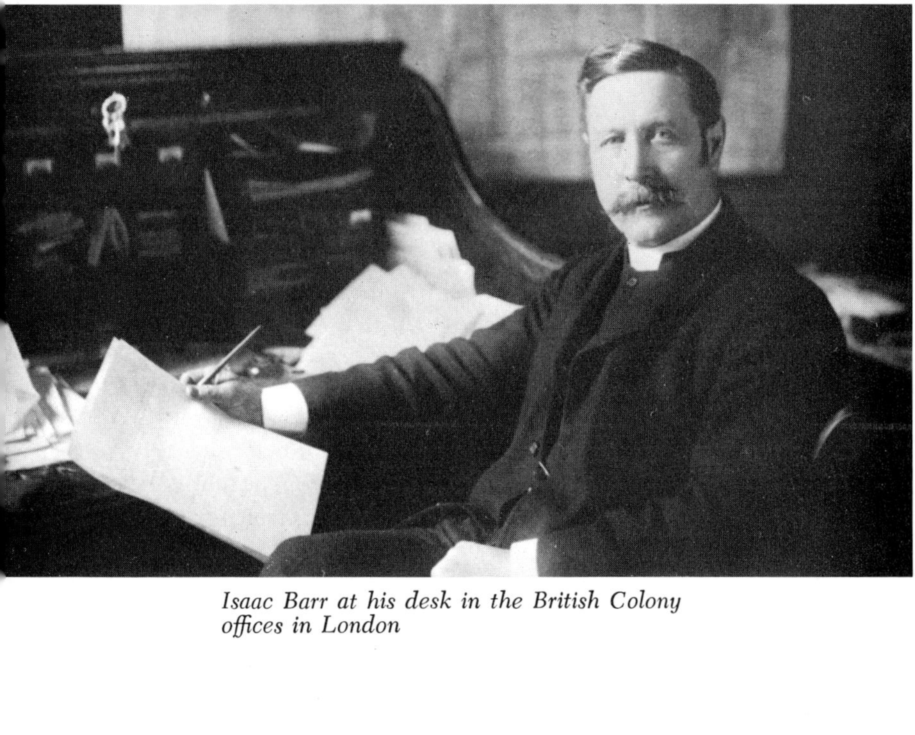

Isaac Barr at his desk in the British Colony offices in London

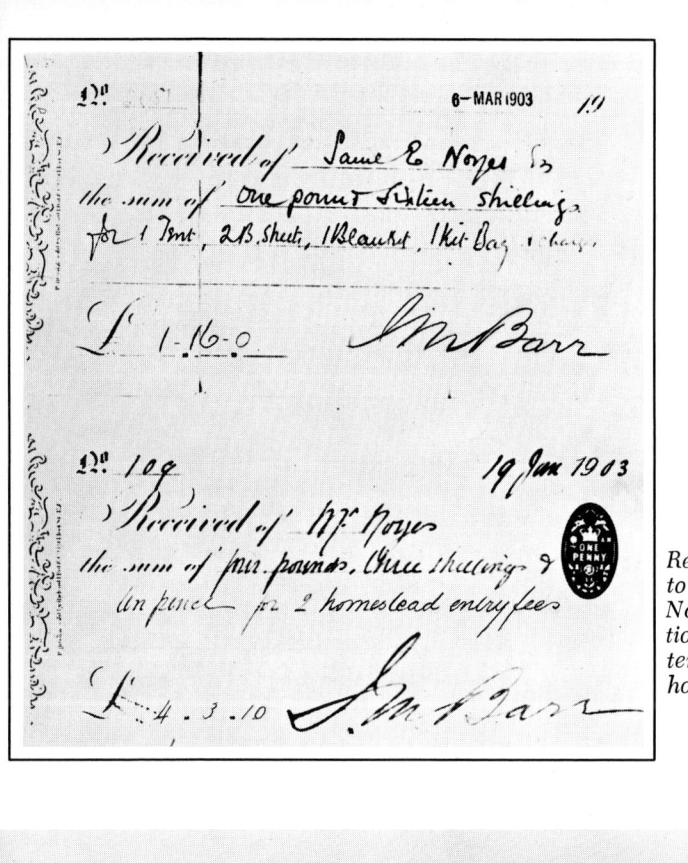

Receipts issued by Isaac B[arr] to S. Noyes (cousin of Alf[red] Noyes, the poet) in conn[ec]tion with purchase of b[ell] tent and blankets and [for] homestead entry fees

SS Lake Manitoba

be large and increasing and they had no intention of giving it up lightly.

Share capital was fixed at seventy-five thousand dollars, a hundred shares at two hundred and fifty dollars each and ten thousand shares at five dollars each, and directors were appointed. A manager experienced in Canadian merchandising was to be selected "by cable," bankers were named and Canadian incorporation would be sought as soon as an advance party reached Winnipeg. Isaac Barr was to be treasurer.[16]

By the end of February he had set about establishing a hospital scheme, Canada's first medicare: "After exhaustive investigation I have come to the conclusion that the principle of insuring against sickness is the one most suitable to my colony." The rates for adults, male and female, were to be five dollars per annum (in maternity cases an extra $12.50 per week would be added), children under fifteen years $2.50 per annum. Family tickets, where over five members were insured, would be at a twenty per cent reduction. Annual tickets entitled the holder to hospital care, medical attendance and nursing, board and lodging; "the only extra will be for medicines, and these will be supplied at wholesale prices."

The matron was already appointed and the equipment was being purchased. The hospital would go directly to Saskatoon where it would be set up in a tent ready to receive patients. It would later move up to the colony. Barr exhorted his people: TAKE TIME BY THE FORELOCK. PURCHASE A TICKET. THE YEAR COVERED BY THE TICKET WILL DATE FROM THE DATE OF ARRIVAL AT SASKATOON. "I shall be personally responsible for the carrying out of the terms of the ticket for I shall be the sole owner of the hospital. The money paid me for the ticket of admission will form a fund by itself to meet all expenses of the hospital, and will establish it on a substantial and permanent basis."[17]

Barr needed the ticket money, for he had no capital either to buy equipment or to hire nurses and doctors. Though it appeared that by joining the scheme one would have complete coverage, except for maternity cases and medicines, some colonists insist it was a ticket of admission only.[18] No matter what the intent, the funding was certainly unsound. The money received for the tickets of admission was used to purchase the hospital tent, beds, blankets and linen, nursing equipment, drugs and supplies. It could not possibly be stretched to cover the salaries of nurses and doctors, far less the daily cost of running a hospital.

THE SASKATOON AND SASKATCHEWAN TRANSPORT COMPANY was the latest syndicate, with capital of fifteen thousand dollars at five dollars per share, and on the board of management, "elected by the shareholders," appeared the name J. B. Barr. This was Jack Barr, Isaac's brother, freighter and horse dealer from the Northwest Plains. Again Isaac was treasurer.[19]

This syndicate seems to have been an attempt to provide transport for the essential services that the colony would require. Someone would have to freight supplies from Saskatoon up to the colony site until the railroad came through. No settler could afford the ten days to two weeks necessary for the return journey. Isaac's brother Jack was already established on the prairies as a horse trader and could enter the freighting business. There were established freighters already but their resources would be inadequate to provide service suddenly to so large a community. Though colonists invested in the stores syndicate and the hospital scheme, I could find no evidence that anyone put money into the transport company.

To add further to the load he carried Isaac, as an agent for railway lands, sent out a prospectus detailing the cost of a section of land on a cash basis or the instalment plan, and accepted these payments so that settlers could purchase additional property adjoining their homesteads.[20]

The sailing had been set for March 25, 1903, and as the time neared Lloyd described the office methods. "He [the secretary] was worried and nervous at the rush of business. Money was coming in for stores, medical shares, blankets, tents, C.P.R. lands, and $10.00 homestead fees."[21] All required receipts. There were the endless enquiries of the colonists to be dealt with; the bookkeeping for the various syndicates and the hospital scheme; the arrangements to be completed with the Canadian government, the shipping agents and railroads on both sides of the ocean; the allotment of homesteads and all the other details that Barr believed only he could attend to. By this time Barr's dreams were beginning to outstrip reality. It is doubtful if he could have accomplished all the things he undertook with a staff ten times the size.

But there was no letting up. For those who could not come with the main party but would join the colony later, he said he was organizing a department to arrange for the erection of houses on homestead land, and to look after the plowing and seeding of at least ten acres on each property for a fee of about five dollars per acre. Further he offered to see that the houses were insured and that posts and rails for fences were delivered onto the land. He did not offer to do these things himself but to hire someone on behalf of the settler to undertake the task.

For an absentee fee of five dollars he agreed to have someone supervise a man's homestead to protect it against depredations and the threat of squatters.[22] It was the misinterpretation of this offer that finally turned the Canadian government officials against him.[23]

Lloyd himself sent a letter to intending colonists announcing that he had engaged a Mr. Herbert Hall, a graduate of Guelph Agricultural College and a practical farmer, who would, for a fee of $1.25 a month or $10.00 per year, instruct and advise inexperienced farmers. He then solicited names for a list of prospective pupils, all to be residents of "*my** township."[24]

On March eleventh the first blow fell. The Elder Dempster Company announced that the sailing would be delayed from March twenty-fifth to March thirty-first and that passengers holding tickets on the *Lake Simcoe* or the *Montrose*

---

*Italics supplied.

previously planned for the Barr colony would be provided berths on the SS *Lake Manitoba*. Barr promptly dispatched a notice to the colonists, stating indignantly that neither the delay nor the doubling up was his doing[25] but obviously this failed to register with them. As migrants tidied up their affairs, disposed of household effects and made their goodbyes, the first small warning of the trouble ahead was clear.

A Pair of Priests

Loading of SS *Lake Manitoba* had been painfully slow that March 31, 1903. This new ship, launched just twenty-one months before, had originally accommodation for 550 passengers.[1] For this trip the forward hold had been fitted up with wooden bunks, one above the other, each provided with a straw mattress but no blankets. This was steerage. Now she would take aboard 1,962 persons with all their personal baggage and household goods for their new life in the Barr Colony.

Lloyd had written to "all the sons of clergy and other young men who have asked to go to my township in Saskatchewan. I shall sail on *Manitoba*. If your ticket is not on that boat you better ask Elder Dempster to transfer you to it, even if you must take third class."[2] (He might have saved himself the trouble. All those booked on the other ships were crowded onto the *Manitoba* anyway.)

The colonists had been pouring into Liverpool for two days.

Now, it was just a medley of all kinds of people around the dock. You never saw such an outfit—a conglomeration of different people with their dogs, their parrots and their umbrellas, their guns and food. And poor old grandmothers crying because their daughters were going away. My father was dead. There was just my mother and seven of us, and they all came down to say goodbye to me. Well, you know how it is. Mother, she started to sing hymns and do a little

praying, hoping I'd be a good boy. Brought tears to my eyes.
I was all overcome.[3]

But a ship must take her tide and her tide had come.
"The last loading was so rushed there was no time for
proper slings into the hold. Great hawsers were thrown
around trunks and boxes and many of them broke open
dumping their contents into the sea, to be lost."[4]

The ship was stern out and as she came about all the passengers rushed to the side to catch the last glimpse of England and hear the last strains of "God Be With You Till We
Meet Again" played by the band ashore. She keeled over
perilously, and the captain on the bridge roared to the mate
below, who was taking her out, "Get those people topside!"
[Or so the story goes.] The unballasted ship rode high and
it was by grace that she made the voyage safely. There was
a paucity of lifeboats, not enough fresh water, inadequate
food.[5]

There was no privacy in the steerage so the women and
children were assigned one area and the men another.
Crowded and poorly ventilated, the "filthy sanitary sur-
roundings" did little to help the seasick as the top-heavy
ship rode the Atlantic swells. The second day out a delega-
tion demanded that the captain put back to the nearest port
and land them. Naturally he refused.[6]

I have to tell you about the food. Maybe the first-class passengers fared better, I was steerage. We had a horrible con-
coction called "ling fish." It was yellow smoked cod and it
smelled to high heaven. That and hardboiled eggs. When
everybody was seated at the table the steward would come
around with a big basket of eggs. I can see it now. He'd start
rolling the eggs down the table and you grabbed an egg as
it went by. Some of those eggs were half-hatched. No bread,
just ship's biscuits, big as a saucer and about half an inch
thick. No butter; they did give us some margarine near the
end. We didn't die but we damned near starved to death![7]

Where were the bills of fare that Barr had promised his
colonists? They invited him down for a meal with them.

"After we ate he was standing on a box so we could all see him, about 400 of us down there. Well, somebody hit him in the face with a ship's biscuit right across the mouth, knocked him off the box. He retreated up the steps calling us a lot of savages. But he was able to improve the food some."[8]

There is no question the passengers were uncomfortable and miserable. The dogs, smelly and sick, roamed among the excess baggage that crowded the deck. The smoking room had been turned into a sort of hospital for the women and children too ill to remain below. Mrs. Lloyd and a volunteer tended them there. "There were two official nurses belonging to the party aboard but they declined to render any help on the ground that their employment did not begin until they reached Saskatoon."[9] That this pair had been hired by Barr did nothing to endear him to the colonists.

"Barr was blamed for all the problems; the overcrowding, the loss of luggage, the poor food; and some of the blame was rightly his. He had undertaken much more than he could deliver; he seemed unable to delegate duty, and he had been too trusting of the word of the steamship company. Day after day he spent in his cabin with his secretary Mr. Flamank struggling with the logistics of moving two thousand people thousands of miles. No businessman, he was just inadequate to do the bookwork necessary because of the expanded numbers. Above all he was remote."[10] Barr's image with the colonists continued to deteriorate.

Meanwhile Lloyd's image rapidly improved. With no direct responsibility for the welfare of the immigrants, he constantly went about the ship. "There would be little knots of people collected around his flat black hat wherever he went on deck, picking his way between piles of excess luggage. They asked him questions, the same questions, over and over again and he kept on answering them. He developed a good rapport with the colonists; he was tactful, he was clear, he was forthright. He projected the image of a leader and it imprinted itself."

The two priests were direct opposites. Lloyd was tall and spare and spoke with a slight lisp. Hard-headed and practical, he had "piercing eyes that seemed to see right through you." A good organizer and administrator, he carried with him a burning missionary zeal. The church was the centre of the community. He refused to take a drink and reproved his parishioners for doing so. Everybody in the colony knew Lloyd.[11]

Barr, on the other hand, was short, heavy-set, about two hundred and twenty-five pounds, and looked businesslike.[12] His voice, to the frequent embarrassment of his hearers, thundered past a wide full moustache. He had given up being a clergyman but continued to wear a clerical collar. This may have been intended to inspire trust among his followers; later it contributed to his downfall.

"The Reverend I. M. Barr the originator of the colony would look more natural in tweeds than in broadcloth. Handling the details of the biggest immigration scheme of late years, the cloth and the clerical cut of his beard seem slightly out of place. He seems a brisk business man, very enthusiastic over a plan which he undoubtedly thinks the best of its kind ever conceived."[13] Most colonists never had any personal contact with Barr, "The Leader"; in fact many had never seen him. When they went to his London office for an interview they were met by Lloyd.[14] And at sea he remained apart. From Saint John he actually travelled to the railhead at Saskatoon not on the colonist trains, as Lloyd did, but later by regular service.

Every morning on the second-class deck and every afternoon on the third-class deck Lloyd gave a series of lectures, followed by a period of questions and answers, on Canadian life and the problems the immigrant colonist might expect: the Canadian monetary system, Canadian laws, railway travel, how to buy food at divisional points, Indians and so forth. And every evening in the hold, down among the tiers of wooden bunks, he held a religious service. "One evening the lights went out and we might have had a serious panic with the crowded condition of the passages, but nobody moved and somebody sang 'Lead Kindly Light' and we all sang until the lights came on again," noted Lloyd.

By the time they were well at sea the passengers had begun to turn to Lloyd, not Barr, with their problems.

Somebody raced after me [wrote Lloyd] saying there was a serious row going on in the dining room and evidently there might be a general fight on hand. . . . I found the large dining room in a state of great excitement some standing on chairs to see and a great crowd gathered in the centre. Here was a tall South African ex-soldier backed by a number of others, evidently ex-soldiers too, and facing him was a little steward (backed by the other stewards) and spattered down his white jacket and trousers a saucerful of jam had been thrown. He was red as a turkey cock and quite ready to fight, soldier or no soldier. There was silence for a minute or two while I stood looking first at the soldier, and then at the little steward. Presently I said to the soldier, "Did you throw that at him?" "Yes," said the soldier, in a tone of voice which indicated that he was quite ready to throw the steward overboard as well. I looked him up and down and then said, "What, a little fellow like that?" (That touched him right on the spot) and I added, "You might at least scrape it off him." In an instant he changed and said, "I will," and he scraped it off clean as he could, and then . . . shook hands with the little steward—and the fight was off.[15]

This was to be the story. More and more the colonists looked to Lloyd and more and more they rejected Barr and his leadership. Of the two, Lloyd was in the better position. He could always say that the problems were Barr's to settle, and this was true. Without assuming the slightest responsibility, Lloyd became the immigrants' support and comforter.

With the end of the voyage came fresh trouble.

When they reached St. John, the ship walked in, and the people were getting madder every minute. They were armed to the teeth, there were hundreds of dogs and they wanted off the ship. But it was Good Friday and a day of waiting. The ship lay anchored out in the stream, for St. John had only limited dockage, and this was a holiday and the unloading crews were not at work. She must wait till a berth was available.[16]

The delay, with land in sight, seemed unbearable to the passengers. On Saturday, two young men from the local bank came aboard to change English pounds for Canadian currency, and did so brisk a business with the well-to-do colonists that within a short time the money-changers had run out of cash. But the next day was Sunday, followed by Easter Monday, a bank holiday, and no more currency would be available. The bankers returned to the town and gathered up what money they could from various sources but it was well into Sunday before all needs were met.

Health inspection proved a further delay. The ship was well at sea by the time the colonists had realized they must be vaccinated before landing. Supplies of vaccine aboard soon gave out. As impatient immigrants lined up for what seemed endless hours waiting to disembark, they quickly learned that by pressing a shilling firmly against the arm for a few minutes, they could make a mark which, as the line filed by the inspector, would pass at a cursory glance for a real vaccination.

The colonists forgot that the unfortunate Good Friday arrival and the delay in landing were not Barr's fault. He had clearly informed them by individual letter before they left England that the change in sailing date was not his doing but that of the steamship company.[17] They forgot that he had arranged for the bankers to come aboard as a convenience to them; that he could have had no way of knowing how much currency they would wish to exchange. They forgot that they were individually responsible for meeting the health regulations. Tired, uncomfortable, impatient, they forgot that Barr had offered them, not the ease of a cruise abroad, but the challenge and hardship of pioneer life.

It was at this point that some five hundred colonists gathered on the after deck to present three hundred dollars to the Lloyds, a gift for the purchase of a pair of horses and a buckboard when they reached the colony.[18] There was no presentation for Barr.

In fact when some CPR officials came aboard to see him on Saturday, according to Lloyd he was nowhere to be found. The rumours flew: Barr had left the ship and was hiding in some local hotel; he had deserted. The officials asked to see Lloyd, who reminded them he was only the chaplain and did not wish to interfere. They said "there would be heavy demurrage for holding the ship and also for the four trains waiting on shore," said Lloyd writing later. It is difficult to understand why they needed Barr at this precise moment, why they did not dock the ship without him; she was still anchored in the river. Surely docking and docking fees were the business of the dockmaster, the steamship company and the captain. This was no concern of Barr; he and his colonists were merely passengers. In fact by the time the ship reached land her ownership had been transferred to the CPR.[19]

"They had the police force, the fire brigade, and a number of railway people looking for I. M. Barr all over the city and he could not be found," continued Lloyd. "I was afraid he had gone to Ottawa without saying a word to us." If they could not find Barr, Lloyd agreed to take over in the morning. Take over what is not clear.

Perhaps the fire brigade did find Barr, though Lloyd suggested later that he did not turn up till number four train was loading, late Sunday evening. In any case the ship docked by 5 A.M. on Easter Sunday morning. The cranes had been at work all night bringing the baggage up from the hold to the deck, and as it was lowered to the dock the noise and confusion, the crowding and impatience mounted to a crescendo. The CPR officials warned that if more baggage were off-loaded the passengers could not be disembarked.

In the minds of the colonists Barr, by his absence, had defaulted. The unloading problems were not his but those of the shipping line, the dock authorities and the railroad, but "The Leader" should have been there to arrange the best possible solution.

In all the confusion Lloyd did the logical thing. He went to the CPR officials. "The C.P.R. was like God in those days." Had the people been held up as the customs officials wanted, they would have been there a couple of weeks clearing their luggage. Then Lloyd came marching back and climbed to the upper deck. He made an impressive sight, standing there where he had held church service that Easter morning: "I've got news for you. The C.P.R. has ordered that the customs inspection be waived. Get all the trains clear of St. John by midnight! This is an order from the C.P.R."[20] It was Lloyd, not Barr, who made the dramatic announcement.

There were four trains. Number one was for single men going as far as Winnipeg, there to seek work for a year before coming up to the colony. It left by 9 A.M. Number two carried single men going as far as Saskatoon and then on to the colony. It got away by noon. The third train left by 6 P.M. and contained families. Number four took aboard all those remaining and pulled away from Saint John before midnight. To speed the dispatch, a baggage train was made up to follow the others, since it was impossible to sort all the colonists' possessions and ensure that they left on the same train with their owners. Just who decided to send the baggage separately is not clear, but Barr paid dearly for that decision.

Lloyd, writing thirty-seven years after the event, described how people who had purchased blankets from Barr in London and needed them on the train journey west were unable to get them because the ship's packer, Jackson, had stored them deep in the hold. On the dock were some piles of blankets belonging to the colony stores syndicate. Under pressure to get the trains on the way, Lloyd issued these blankets to the colonists, each receiving the number they claimed they had bought from Barr. He kept a list of the colonists' names, and they were to return these blankets to the store when they received those they had purchased from Barr before sailing.

We had finished about two thirds of the number four train when I heard a voice say over my shoulder, "What are you doing with my blankets?" I turned and saw I. M. Barr with a very white face and fierce eyes looking just like a spirit drunk man. I was angry and said, "Why were you not here to look after this yourself? This is not my work. But where were you? These people have paid you for the blankets and they cannot get them. They cannot travel without the blankets. . . ." He was still blurting out, "They are my blankets, I cannot afford to give them away." [Nor could he.] I threw the papers down on the seat and said, "There are the lists, now finish it yourself," and off I went in an angry mood.[21]

Barr may very well have been absent from the ship for some time on Saturday, as Lloyd claimed. But the two priests granted an interview to a reporter from the *Toronto News* during a luncheon aboard,[22] outlining their plans for the colony. Number four train, which left at midnight Sunday, was loading when the blanket incident is said to have occurred. Taken together, this could mean Barr was absent from Saturday evening to Sunday evening.[23]

And he may have been drunk when he returned to the dock. Isaac Barr, like his father before him, did drink. The colonists differ on the subject. Some deny he was ever drunk[24, 25] and one told me that when he bought a blanket from Barr on the dock, "He was so inebriated he was unable to make the proper change."[26] Whether Barr was drunk on Easter Sunday on the dock at Saint John will likely never be known. Of itself the point is of no importance but as a background for Lloyd's implacable hatred of Barr it is significant, for Lloyd abhorred all drinking.

The writing in Lloyd's memoirs is carefully worded. "Before long the C.P.R. officials came back and said, with the captain to help them they had pushed I. M. Barr off the train and that he was now locked up in his cabin on the ship." Just what was the Reverend George Exton Lloyd saying? That the captain and the officials had locked Barr up? In the captain's cabin? Or did he mean that Barr had retired to his own cabin and locked his door? Later in the memoir Lloyd says, "He [Barr] forgot all about the arrangement (made with the doctors) or else he was peeved about the incident of the issue of his blankets to the people on the trains, or about his being locked in his cabin on the ship until after our #4 train left St. John."[27]

Barr was a gentle man who would go out of his way to avoid a quarrel[28] but Lloyd does not spare him.

The last thing I have to record about the voyage is not so pleasant. It was just before we reached the harbour of St.

John. Mr. Barr had bought up all the flour that was left in the ship and got the bakers to make it into loaves, to be sold to the settlers just before they began the journey on the trains. That might have been a very helpful move, one that would have been remembered with thanks. But the price was put at ten cents a loaf. One of the ship's officers said that it was not the right price because we could get all we wanted at five cents when we landed in St. John.

But could they? Saint John was not prepared for the influx. It was the Easter holiday and the stores were closed, their supplies already depleted by the residents stocking up. The bakers of Saint John would not know either the precise time of the ship's arrival or how many would want bread. When the matter was called to Barr's attention he reduced the price to five cents. "But it was too late! Everybody was talking about it and suggesting that I. M. Barr 'was on the make!' "[29] If Barr was on the make at this time he was an amateur, for the whole deal would have netted him a paltry twenty-five to thirty dollars. Whether he actually knew he was overcharging is not mentioned in Lloyd's retrospect.

Barr was quick-tempered and undiplomatic. "He had to go it alone — that was his nature, he couldn't delegate duty,"[30] and as his arrangements gradually fell apart and his promises faded the colonists became bitter with disillusion.

The trains were slow running over the single-track line, with innumerable stops by the "specials" to let ordinary traffic go through. These were neither British commuter trains nor the *Flying Scotsman*. During the waits on the sidings the colonists would wander into the fields with their guns to shoot at the gophers and rabbits. One colonist on train three described a hold-up near Portage La Prairie:

"There were an awful lot of antelope crossing the track. About 5,000 I suppose. We all looked out to see what was stopping the train—no station here. You can imagine what it was like to see all those green Englishmen seeing all those antelope. They just stood still and stared. Not one of them fired a shot though they had regular arsenals with them. You would have thought they were going out to fight the Indians."[31]

In Winnipeg some of the passengers in number three train had gone up to the town to buy food, and the specials, running on no regular schedule, left without them. The obliging railway company got out a coach and engine and chased up the line with the latecomers to dump them on the already overcrowded number four.

To an Englishman accustomed to the compartmented cars of the British railways Canadian colonist cars were crude affairs, and though they had been accurately described in the pamphlets he simply could not picture them as they were. "There were bunks up on the wall. They pulled down on a chain, you know. No mattresses. There was a stove at one end of each car for anybody who cared to cook. No diners on the train. No food. There would be several families on a single car. There were more fights! At last we appointed a steward, and he would give each family so long to have the stove, but it wasn't very satisfactory."[32]

That the little station stores *en route* were unable to cope with the needs of two thousand people in transit was Barr's fault—or so the travellers said, as they whiled away the long hours, confined, uncomfortable, weary and often apprehensive. And perhaps it was, for he had trusted the railroad people to see to these things; they, not he, would know where the stops were to be made. The railway officials did take care to see that the colonists were not overcharged by the wayside suppliers. It was not that the colonists suffered for anything; it was just that it was all so different from Britain: no cities, no shops, no porters, no sheets, no mattresses, no "cuppa."

The national press followed the progress of the party across Canada with straight news stories and interviews with Barr and Lloyd. The former had stopped off in Ottawa.

Think of it, he [Barr] said in a brief interview snatched from the press of work, 1,900 here, 1,500 more to follow shortly, and 10,000 more coming next year. And all British, and everyone taking up land in your west. All have paid their homestead fees in advance and in addition many have bought large quantities of railway land on speculation. Most of those you see are men of large means and all of them have money. About £500,000 sterling is represented aboard. All kinds and conditions of men are represented, from the Oxford man down to the small farmer and artisan. We have in this party five earls' nephews, several capitalists, many clergymen, lawyers, doctors and whatnot.[33]

Barr was carried away. All but one hundred and seventy-six listed their occupations: no doctors, but one herbalist and one dentist; one solicitor, a couple of teachers, one clergyman, a missionary bound for Calgary in addition to Barr and Lloyd, a few accountants, secretaries. The earls' nephews failed to declare themselves; in fact there was no place on the application for this type of information. But of the non-dependants, the family heads and earners, twenty-eight per cent had been either farmers or in associated trades: dairymen, gardeners, horsemen.[34]

We hope to keep the colony as far as possible free from any foreign admixture, even of American people, for, though I have the most friendly feelings toward the United States, I think it is not wise to mix that people with this colony. I hope to keep it British in actuality as well as sentiment.

We have already established a store at Saskatoon from which point the 150 mile trek to Battleford begins, and a store is being opened at the other end. We are bringing with us the materials for opening stores of all kinds. We will have a hospital furnished with medicines . . . and provided with three nurses. [Barr had just engaged two Montreal doctors by phone to join the party.] Each settler on payment of a pound will get the benefits of this hospital. We propose to establish a bank and will advance credit to those settlers who stand in need of it. We have secured the contract from the Canadian Northern Railway to construct one hundred miles through our settlement. This will furnish employment to those who want it and put money into circulation. We have bought a herd of cattle and a large number of horses. We will keep up a service by means of teams between Saskatoon and the colony until a railroad has been built. With respect to the mode of laying out the colony the natives of each county will be placed together. Thus all the Somerset-shire people will be placed alongside one another, the same for the Surrey people and so on. It is the solidarity and purely British character of the colony that attracts the people.[35]

Confident as he sounded, there were uneasy signs. On April sixth, even before the colonists had landed, Mr. W. S. Bromhead, agent for the Barr Colony had wired from Saskatoon to Winnipeg to detain the colonists for a few days until supplies ordered came forward. "The tents for the Barr colonists are up but the stoves needed have not arrived."[36]

Even while Barr was giving his interview in Ottawa the *Saskatchewan Herald,* the voice of Battleford, trumpeted this warning:

The fulfilment of Mr. Barr's promises to his people being apparently abandoned . . . it would be wise for the colonists to take matters in their own hands while there is time and before they have exhausted their means. The plan of the colony as outlined in the English pamphlet was alright as far as colonies go, but in the absence of the faintest attempt to carry it out there can be nothing but disaster. The stores syndicate that was to have supplied all the neces-saries of life has fallen to pieces, and the goods are not likely to get beyond Saskatoon. Whatever has been done towards receiving them and transporting them has been done by the government, but it cannot undertake to do for them all that Mr. Barr promised. . . . The Syndicate that was to have fur-nished transportation for women and children to the des-tination has also gone out of existence. All these sideshows that have been depending on Mr. Barr for money are out of funds . . . neither has the sawmill that was to have furnished them with lumber been put in evidence. Under the circum-stances we would advise the colonists to withdraw from the colony, take up land within reach of neighbours, civilization and supplies. To continue in a party where every advantage conferred is measured by the amount of commission it will yield the managers is courting disaster, and this we would avert as far as we are able.[37]

But the editor was only partly right. Though his advice to the colonists to take up land closer to neighbours and suppliers was good, his claims that Barr had defaulted were wrong. In Saskatoon the tents were already up; the syndicate store was in operation.[38] The transport company, in which no one invested, never did function. Perhaps because of this Barr had to make other plans. The same paper recorded that in mid-February, a month before the party sailed, Barr's agents had arranged with the government for overland transportation.[39] This was confirmed in the government agent's report to Lord Tennyson's Committee. Mr. C. W. Speers, the government agent, also stated that he had arranged for the sawmill. And it did go into operation.[40] The editorial with its warnings and doubts could only undermine what confidence the colonists had in Barr.

The three trains (number one had gone only as far as Winnipeg) arrived in Saskatoon on Saturday, April eighteenth, to be greeted by Mr. Speers, who made a little speech of welcome to the colonists, who rushed from the train but were persuaded to line up on the platform. There were cheers for the Canadian government, Speers and Lloyd, but for Barr groans. He was still in Ottawa and not there to hear them.

Saskatoon was only a small village but the prairie land boom had already begun. There were several general stores, a harness shop, two small hotels, a hardware and an implement shop, a bakery, a lumber mill and a flour mill and some scattered small houses. The resources of the little community were already overtaxed by the thousands of American and European settlers heading west for the free-grant lands.

The tent city had been erected on the banks of the Saskatchewan River, a brown stream swollen with the spring run-off rushing between banks piled high with the great ice blocks left by the break-up.

When the last train arrived the families streamed off, each member carrying a load of cooking utensils and boxes, lugging blankets and portmanteaus, piling them up in one spot until they got a tent to cover them. These were bell tents, purchased by Barr from the army surplus of the Boer War and sold to the settlers at five dollars each.

". . . jolly good value they were for $5 though the people objected to paying $1 for transportation to the site. The blankets were horrible, some blighter at the war office had put them over on Barr. Nothing in this area was overcharged."[41] The small metal stoves of Russian manufacture were good and reasonable.

Sanitary facilities were meagre, a hole in the ground with a piece of canvas stretched around for a screen. Drinking water was scarce—a few small wells in the main portion of the camp.

The horse tents were the real business district of the huge Barr community, whether it was for deals of land or stock or for the labours of the members of the colony.

England had been transplanted. Social distinctions were sharply defined. At the "South End" of the canvas town were the hospital, Barr's tent (a structure divided by canvas partitions to form office and living quarters)[42] and the tents of the more wealthy newcomers whose ladies put on afternoon dress and paid afternoon calls. "Here the men affect horsiness or sportiness of attire, whipcord breeches, leather leggings, sombreros and ties that wake the echoes, and stroll around camp with setters and pointers at heel, exhibiting to admiring friends their 'hammerless or Savage.' A stroll through this section of the camp towards evening is like ladies day at Westpoint [sic] or Bisley."[43]

The Lieutenant-Governor, in a letter to Barr welcoming the colonists, congratulated him on his choice of site and added that he himself was an example of what lay ahead once they had overcome their first difficulties. They should take hope, he said.[44] And aim to become lieutenant-governors? That his name spelt Forget must have held some sort of portent for many.

The stores syndicate had set up in the main portion of the camp and was doing a brisk business.

The big marquee was fitted with rough lumber counters and stocked with everything from butchers meat to axehandles.

Almost everything necessary to start work on a farm can be procured through this store, and generally speaking at reasonable prices—far more reasonable the colonists state than at the stores in town. The arrangement and display of goods would certainly not commend itself to a city merchant. The boxes, barrels and crates in which the goods were shipped were roughly broached open, and their contents exposed to view. Rows of shovels, hay and stable forks leaned against the wall, a stack of brooms stood against one corner and another of campstoves was stacked outside. Barrels of coal-oil and piles of bread were grouped in various parts of the tent, and behind the counters every imaginable kind of canned commodity was displayed. A half dozen clerks were busy handing out goods. Of mercantile courtesy, little was shown. The clerks were too busy and the customers too eager. Surrounding the big trading marquee are several other tents used for storing supplies. These are crowded with goods but are rapidly being depleted under the steady demand.[45]

"Barr agents have established restaurants where meals can be purchased at a quarter each. Over in the village, until the arrival of the dining crew, meals were one dollar apiece."[46]

In the horse tents the help of his brother, Jack Barr, did the Reverend Isaac no good at all. Jack was the regular horse dealer of the times, tough, real tough, and he had undertaken to have four hundred horses at Saskatoon for sale to the colonists. He had shipped in thirty-four head in three carloads, in anticipation of the demand. All those in one car, sixteen head, had suffocated and were dead on arrival, a tremendous loss to Isaac who was already short of money.

Oxen were a hundred and seventy-five dollars a pair and "teams ranged in price from $200 to $450 depending on size and age."

They weren't supposed to be over nine years of age but I know some of those animals must have been with Noah when he came out of the ark. . . . One of the settlers fancied himself a horseman, and he asked Jack Barr for a really good team. "Well," Jack Barr says, "I've got a good pair on the farm, not in here, but I could bring them in tomorrow, and if you have a mind to pay the price you can have them. These horses have been running on the range all winter among the straw stacks and they don't look very good, but they are a good pair of horses and I can guarantee them. They look rough, and maybe you won't think they look very smart but I can guarantee them." Well, the next day, Jack Barr brought the team in and the settler bought them and started to lead them to his wagon by the halter shanks. But they kept stumbling and tripping over the tent ropes, and one of his neighbours said to the new owner, "Can't see very good, can they? Seems like you have bought a pair of blind horses." The owner was mad as a hatter and he went to see Jack Barr the next morning. "Here are your horses, give me my money back or I will have the law on you. You sold me a pair of blind horses!" And Barr replied, "What's wrong with you? I told you they were blind. I told you those horses don't look too good. And you told me that you knew horses and I couldn't fool you on a horse. Now I didn't try to fool you at all. I told you the truth. Now just remember the first man you met in Canada was a real horse trader!"[47]

A man who knew the Barr brothers told me: "I don't think the Reverend Barr was a crook, seemed like a nice man. Spoke like an Englishman. You never knew such a difference between two brothers. Jack Barr was slim and spoke like an American. He was a real tough horse trader and cowpuncher, real hard. He was married to an educated woman, well she had some education. She had one child but Jack Barr wasn't the father, it was by another marriage. She wasn't an Indian but she had some Indian blood in her, a little. Jack lived in Montana, then Battleford."[48]

I had heard the story that followed from several sources:

There was Ed Salsbury. He was a telegraph operator at a little station about 25 miles from Saskatoon. Salsbury lived alone and had this beautiful horse and he sure liked it. He came up to Battleford, got drinking with Jack Barr, got real drunk and traded horses with him. After he sobered up he went to Barr to get his horse back, but Jack Barr only laughed at him. He offered to buy the horse back but Barr still laughed. Well, Barr was having a drink at the bar and Salsbury pulled out a six-gun and started shooting. One bullet went through the pewter mug that Barr had up to his mouth. The bullet stayed in the mug. When the shooting began everyone started to run out. They tripped over the guy ropes of the marquee that the colonists had put up beside the hotel and fell all over. I was there. I saw it all and then I got out too.[49]

It was a good story and I wondered if it was true. It must have been six months after I heard it that, when reading through accounts describing the scene at Battleford and the location of the colonists' marquee, I suddenly knew the incident had happened. The tent was just outside the door of the bar! And the patrons, in full flight, would quite likely have stumbled over the ropes.

Englishmen are accustomed to looking after their own luggage. The colonists took with them what they could find at the dockside and had reluctantly consented to the remainder, along with the large pieces shipped as settlers' effects, being loaded onto the baggage cars to follow them to Saskatoon. Naturally, railways being what they are, these pieces would not be there when the passengers arrived. In fact one carload was shunted off to the United States. In any case there was no freight-handling facility at the railhead capable of dealing with a shipment this size. Barr had asked his agent, Mr. Bromhead, to have a large tent by the track for the baggage but it was not there. The railroad officials promptly off-loaded the crates, trunks and pianos onto the open prairie. Barr tried to protect their possessions by having each owner identify his own property in an orderly manner, and then sign a waiver freeing the railway of responsibility for this unchecked baggage. This infuriated the Englishmen, anxious to claim their possessions. They threatened to charge. Barr made the mistake of threatening them back—with the police. The colonists fought their way to the railside and seized their own. And damned Barr.

> Barr, Barr, wily old Barr,
> He'll do you as much as he can.
> You bet he will collar
> Your very last dollar,
> In the valley of the Sask-atch-ewan.[50]

For the unhappy disgruntled followers, the fact that there was a lot of baggage missing, that they had let it out of their sight, that they were sure it was lost forever, made them blame Isaac all the more. It was another defeat. Barr had been trying to protect his people's possessions in a situation, not of his making, not his responsibility but the CPR's. The breach between "The Leader" and his colonists was now irreparable.

His transport plans were also teetering. That too had been left to Jack Barr, who persuaded about thirty or forty Indians and Métis to come in from nearby reservations with horses and wagons. The government too had called in freighters. The rate, three to three and a half dollars per hundredweight from railhead to colony site, seemed prohibitive to the colonists. But the trip took ten days; the maximum load per trip would be a ton—and Isaac had made it plain before they left England that this service would cost them something.[51]

By this time it was obvious that about eighty colonists had less than fifty dollars and of these about ten had families. One young Englishman, after the purchase of a yoke of oxen and a breaking-plow, would have about thirty-five dollars to last him a year. His slender, dark-eyed wife, romantic to the core, dreamed of frontier life.

She would cook and sew in this far Canadian valley, and fight shoulder to shoulder with her husband to the goal of fortune. . . . She could hear her . . . friends saying to each other: "There goes the pluckiest little woman in town. She went away out to Canada where there were polar bears, wildcats, wolves, Indians and crocodiles and things and helped him to get a fortune."

"What am I going to do for food, for a house and barns and horses and all the other implements?" the husband wanted to know.

"Why hire yourself out to break sod for Mr. Barr."

"But I cannot break sod, doncher know. I never did it before."

"You could learn."

"And where will I live?"

"Build a sod house."

"What's that? . . . I don't think I could possibly do it."

"Yes you could . . . take your stuff out there. Make some money carrying another man's goods along with yours."

"Whom shall I get to drive the oxen?"

"Drive 'em yourself!" This almost dumbfounded the Englishman. A little while later his wife announced that she would become a Ruth of the Wilderness. "I shall go out and bustle in the harvest field with my dear husband." That is the type of one of the women who are going out to pioneer life, to mother the next generation of a young country.[52]

A reporter described the church service that first Sunday in camp:

"The wilderness and the solitary place shall be glad for them and the desert shall rejoice and blossom as the rose," read the minister [the local clergyman]. He knew. He had travelled over these lonely plains two score years, facing the bitter blasts of a northwest winter, christening, baptizing and performing the last rites of his church. The drone of prayers and the rippling congregational response of the English Church Service came from the big dining tent today. The tent was crowded. Ladies in fine tailor made suits, dainty hats, and neatly gloved bowed their heads in prayer, with men in broadcloth and tweed, clean linen, white ties or hunting stocks. Shoes were neatly polished and only a gay sweater or two, and the gay neckerchief of the cowpunchers, who strayed curiously in, betrayed the situation. It would not be hard to imagine outside, the resident grass and sparkling sea of an English watering place. Instead in the sunlight lay the yellow prairie with sloughs glittering in the sunshine. The day's lesson was particularly appropriate; the rebellion of Korah against Moses as told in Numbers was read. "Moreover thou hast not brought us up out of a land flowing with milk and honey to kill us in the wilderness, except thou make thyself altogether a prince over us."

What kind of people was this that came into the wilderness with top hats? There is the trouble. Some are too luxurious. Many of those who came in by the last train are making ill feeling by superior airs. They are the bathtub, piano carrying fellows, and unconsciously the disturbing element. They have money to purchase cattle, implements and provide transport for their multitudinous boxes and portmanteaux, and those who have less are a trifle jealous and envious.[53]

By Wednesday the colonists held a mass meeting to protest the high prices charged by the local merchants. Some money found its way to Barr, they claimed. The prairie storekeepers knew a good thing when they saw it and naturally wanted to make what they could out of the colonists before they, in their large numbers, moved on. Besides, the merchants resented the stores syndicate, and Barr's attitude that it was best to keep the profits within the colony. As it was, estimates say that drafts for $250,000 to $300,000 were cashed in Saskatoon, that tiny town of a few hundred people and a handful of commercial enterprises.[54]

Barr, who hated a quarrel, would not attend the meeting at first but finally Lloyd persuaded him, and suggested he explain to the people that he must have some money to meet expenses, and they would understand. Isaac stood on a large box and addressed the crowd. He admitted that he had commissions from the steamship company and the railroad, that he had bought some things by outright purchase, like tents, blankets, stoves, but he denied asking the Saskatoon merchants for commissions for directing trade to them. (It would seem folly to recommend that the colonists shop anywhere but in their own stores syndicate.) He ended his speech with a biblical quotation: "Ye must not muzzle the ox which treadeth out the corn." The newspaper accounts of the meeting say that the crowd, excited and eager to question Barr, were diverted by resolutions of thanks to the government and the Canadian Pacific Railway,[55] but Lloyd in his retrospect says: "A man in the middle interrupted him and asked if he had written this letter (holding it up). Was that Mr. Barr's signature?" Barr asked that the letter be passed to him. The man refused and read the letter, "demanding from the storekeepers in Saskatoon a percentage on all the sales to the British colony people. This started an uproar and Barr shouted something that sounded like denying he had signed any such letter!" The colonists brought the letter to Lloyd. "I said I was not an expert in handwriting but they said, 'You must have seen his signature times enough to recognize it.' And the letter was passed forward. All I could say was 'It looks like it.' . . . In the tumult that followed Barr went away. Someone shouted for me so I took the box and urged everyone to take to the trail."[56]

Again Barr had retreated. In a moment of emotion and high drama Lloyd had assumed the leadership.

The Barr Colony

" 'The trail is a good one and the road well bridged,' says Barr. Well, of course there is no such thing as a road as we know it in England. Two wheel marks across the prairies, over sloughs and mountains and across creeks,"[1] wrote a colonist to his girl friend in England.

It is true that the colonists had been warned that the prairies were vast and empty but, accustomed as they were to the little farms of England with ancient roads and tidy hedgerows, they were totally unable to picture the trail to the colony.

Marquees had been set up at intervals of twenty miles to provide shelter and accommodation for those without tents. Stoves, firewood, hay for feeding the animals were all at hand, as Barr had promised, though it was the government which actually provided them, at his request. That the travellers left at irregular times, that they could not manage their horses or slow-moving oxen, that some became stuck or overturned their loads made arrival at these way stations each evening uncertain. Any plans Barr may have had for providing fresh meat at the stops were impractical, without refrigeration and without any knowledge of how many might reach the stop and when. One family could not eat an entire steer.

There were both real and imagined hazards on the trail. Prairie fires, great sheets of flame rushing toward the terrified colonists who took refuge by driving their wagons into the nearby sloughs, left the land black and desolate. Many were afraid of wolves and had visions of themselves fighting to the death against bands of Indians, and so they carried arms to protect them from these menaces. The nights were cold for people inadequately clothed and sheltered only in tents. To some it was an adventure, but to others a misery that set them wondering why they had ever left England. As they journeyed on each hardship became Barr's fault.

How difficult, actually, was the trail to Battleford? Compared to the thousands of miles travelled by the early American and Canadian settlers, really threatened by Indians fearing to be dispossessed, and by wild animals and by outlaws, it was an easy five-day trip. But to the inexperienced Englishman, fresh from crowded England with its buildings, transport, shops and pubs, it was a fearful journey. He looked to Barr who, he was sure, had promised him not only a hundred and sixty acres and a challenge but comforts as well. And when they were lacking he scrawled on the wayside tents with charcoal, *Barr, Barr, Black Sheep* and *We are Barr's Lambs, going to the Promised Land.*[2]

Some even found humour in their plight.

My partners and I wanted a cow so we could have milk to drink and raise calves and things on the farm. Old Tom Dewan, a half-breed at Battleford brought us a big burly range cow with a calf. (*This cow will be alright once she gets away from the herd. Thirty-five dollars, cow and calf. And when she quiets down she'll make a good cow for you. Thirty-five dollars.*)

Well, that seemed reasonable enough so we paid him the money and tied her to the wagon-box cleats under the axle with a rope around her horns. (*She may do a little fighting but after a while she'll be alright.*)

Well, we hitched up and started off. The cow wouldn't lead and there was no way to get her to lead. We even tried twisting her tail. She'd just plant her feet on the ground and shake her head and pull the rope taut as could be. One of the boys decided he was going to get some milk out of her anyway so he sat down and tried. With one kick she landed him and the pail upside down. He was an awful mess. We tried to pull her along but she wouldn't come and the horses were played out pulling against her.

So we got the happy idea of putting the calf on top of the wagon and then turning the cow loose and she would follow. The next thing was to catch the calf. When the old cow saw the four of us chasing the calf around the wagon she went wild, trying to upset the box with her head and trying to get at us. We chased that calf round the wagon till our tongues hung out but eventually we caught him—big strong calf—and pulled him on top of the wagon and tied him there. Then I got under the wagon and chopped the rope to free the old cow. Dassn't get near enough to untie her. She had a couple of big horns she would put right through you.

Well, then the fun started. When the cow found she was loose and the calf was on top of the wagon she just kept up a steady run, round and round, trying to get at the calf and chasing us. She chased us up on top of the wagon too. We darn't come down, she'd make a bee-line for us. We held a council. We knew we'd never get down to even hitch the horses up, no matter how far we went. So we let the calf down to the ground and turned it loose. The pair of them headed back to Battleford. The old cow had our $35 tied to her tail and away she went.[3]

This tale was told me by a colonist who appeared on the passenger list of the SS *Lake Manitoba* as a "farmer"!

The advance hospital, a tent with three cots, had reached Battleford. The main hospital, with two doctors, three nurses and the general equipment, was to come up with Barr from Saskatoon. The agricultural hall had been fitted up with stoves and lamps and a large tent, thirty by ninety feet, contained a good supply of hay and forage.

A few of the settlers turned back. "Somehow everything seemed to be going wrong. You see, my blessed mules were green, you couldn't hold them back with the ropes on their horns. My wife wanted to turn back all the time. I've been wet to the skin for three days. Two of my youngsters have the whooping cough. Barr had $175 of my capital which I said goodbye to of course and, blow me, if I hadn't found out at Saskatoon that Barr had given the other three homesteads in our section to two Welshmen and a Lancashire man."[4] This last was unendurable.

Barr had promised in his pamphlets that people who wished to could settle together, that he would allot homesteads in such a way that families would be near their friends and those from the same county in Britain. Young men would be placed near Mr. Herbert Hall, the farm instructor hired by Lloyd, from whom they might receive instruction for a fee.

Many of these allotments were made before sailing or on board ship, and while the surveyor's map shows little hills and valleys, woods and water,[5] neither Barr nor anyone else could possibly know each section of each township. He had an overall plan, but he reiterated that those who were not satisfied were free to change, without further charge, to a property within or without the colony reservation.[6]

Some colonists arrived ahead of Barr and were determined to settle at once, regardless of the plan. He should have been there to prevent the delay. While R. I. Chisholm, the Dominion Land Agent at Battleford, temporized about accepting their claims, the telegrams flew between Chisholm, Barr and Smart, the Deputy Minister of the Interior.[7] Barr seemed panicky, Smart waffled and Chisholm tried to hold off the squatters. The one man particularly named in the exchange was Penley. There is someone of that name on the directorate of the stores syndicate and he was to have come out early to purchase supplies.

Barr gave a small slip of paper to those to whom he had assigned property indicating its position on the survey. When the colonist reached the headquarters camp he presented this to the land guide who located the place for him.

The colonists pushed on from Battleford—on up to the colony another fifty to sixty miles. Barr had sent ahead a man called Lachlan Taylor to locate the site and put up a big tent there to house the stores.[8] The government had erected two more, one for the colonists and one for the land agents and guides—this was the colony. The newcomer was appalled:

Have you any idea what 160 acres means to an Englishman? He probably never saw 160 acres all at once. I had the idea that farms were just nice little places laid out with a road past them, and some improvements. Maybe not houses, but some improvements so you would know where you were going. We had four quarters, the four of us. There was a dug hole at each of the corners of the section and a stake in the middle, and that showed us where the centre of the section was. And you go so many yards one way and so many the other and that's how you find out where your stakes are. So there you are and the land guide says, "You are located on your land now: 25/50/27." No semblance of roads or anything else. "Now there you are, boy," he said. "Get busy and build your house, put in your garden and look after your horses and you will do all right," and away he went. You are abandoned.

You can imagine what it is like if you are told to build a house and you don't know anything about it. You build a house or freeze to death. So we hitched up the horses to the plow and plowed a long strip of sod. Then we cut the strip in about two-foot lengths, put them on a stoneboat which we made out of logs and hauled them to the site where we were going to build the house, just on a piece of bald prairie. Then you pile up the sods, one atop the other, up to about six to eight feet with some upright poles to hold them. Then you lay poles across the top from wall to wall and cover them with more sods. I suppose our house would be about 16 x 20 feet, or something like that. Mind you, it leaked like the very devil. And the sods kind of settle with the rain so the roof sinks down some.

A sod house is an awfully dirty place to live, but some of us put a floor in. We sawed up poplar logs to about nine-inch blocks and stood them on end close together all over the floor and packed dirt in between them. No doors or windows. We did put the odd bottle we had, plastered into the sod for light. At the door we just made a wooden frame of poplar poles and fastened a gunny sack over it. That was all we had. We couldn't buy any doors. We made beds of poplar poles and threw a little hay on that. With maybe a Barr blanket on top.[9]

There was no post office. Some mail had been dumped on the floor of the stores tent, and the colonists were expected to paw through it to find any addressed to them. Barr had applied to the government to have himself appointed postmaster four days after the general trek westward from Battleford had begun.

Because of the constant threat of squatters, and because many intending colonists could not come out to Canada with the main party or had stopped behind in Winnipeg or Saskatoon to find work until they could afford to take up their land, Barr offered to act as their agent, to file for their homesteads. Requests for this service were made on forms supplied by the Department of the Interior.[10] This was no "Barr scheme" but regular government practice. However, in addition he undertook to see that the property was not usurped by squatters. For this supervision he charged a fee of five dollars. The offer was his undoing with the government.

Mr. Smart, the Deputy Minister, called it an outrage, a direct contravention of the terms under which Barr had had the reservation made for the colony. He thundered that Mr. Barr had been expressly forbidden to charge anyone a fee for joining the colony.[11] Obviously Mr. Smart had not read what Barr undertook for this fee: to hire men "to look after these unoccupied homesteads. . . . I shall take the very greatest care to protect their interests at every point, and to prevent damage to property or unlawful occupation of the same."[12] The absentee fee was in no sense a fee for the privilege of joining the group.

The tent town at Saskatoon was all but deserted just two weeks after the colonists landed in Saint John. They had travelled five days by train to Saskatoon, had been outfitted in about ten days and had taken to the trail. Just three weeks after landing, the first general movement — thirty wagons — left Battleford for the colony site, and the exodus went steadily on, so that most were on their homesteads about a month after landing in Canada.

The Lloyds remained behind in Saskatoon where several of the colonists with pneumonia were in the tent hospital. Several others suffering from scarlet fever occupied a nearby house set up as an isolation centre.[13] After the ship

Barr Colonists leaving Saskatoon for colony site

*River transportation from Edmonton to Hewitt's Landing,
north of Lloydminster; on arrival the barges were broken
up for lumber*

William Hall Barr

William Hall Barr and his wife Phyllis

Christina Helberg Barr and her children Harry Montgomery Baird Barr and William Hall Barr

landed Barr had engaged, by telephone, two Montreal doctors, Amos and Keating, to accompany the party and settle in the colony. Keating remained in Saskatoon to look after the sick and Amos joined Barr and Flamank for the trip to Battleford and the colony, along with the "Women's Ox Transport Train and Stores" which left Saskatoon on May second.

Christina Helberg was with that wagon train too although no one seems to have noted the fact. Unless it was McCormick in *Lloydminster* when he describes how Norman McDonnell, fired by the rumours that spread up and down the trail that Barr intended to desert the colony, that the police had orders to detain him, set out back down the trail to demand a reckoning. McDonnell could not wait for his team and slow-moving outfit. He walked, enquiring of each group of colonists he met if they had seen Barr. Eventually he was able to obtain a horse and saddle and rode for Battleford. Unable to find Barr at either the Queen's or the Albion Hotel, he picked up some encouragement, some liquor and a gun, and continued his pursuit. Finally he came upon the transport train making camp for the night. He spied Barr. Touching him heavily on the shoulder with the gun he demanded the return of the money he had given him for railroad lands. "Barr while for the moment flurried, to know what it all meant, quickly tumbled to the position and put up his hands in a deprecating way as though this gun business were not necessary at all."[14]

McDonnell obviously became impatient and fired a shot. There was a brief scuffle. Then, as colonists gathered outside the tent, Barr spread papers and deeds on the floor and "paid over the disputed money in full." The author says the "single dip" which lighted this scene was held and sheltered from the wind by a woman. He suggested she was Miss Posthuma, a colonist, but it was probably Christina, the London clerk-secretary, going to the colony with Isaac.

Whether she ever reached the site I cannot say, but I believe she got at least as far as Battleford. There, while the agricultural hall served as shelter for the colonists, a large tent in charge of Jack Barr and Robert Reesor provided shelter for the horses and their fodder. Robert Reesor was Isaac's bother-in-law from Markham,[15] on the outskirts of Toronto.

Dissatisfaction among the colonists was mounting and McDonnell had appeared to threaten Isaac's life. It was at this time that Barr offered Dr. Amos a gun and asked him for protection.[16] Likely too at this time he made the decision to send Christina back to Ontario to the care of his sister Jennie, Mrs. Robert Reesor. There she remained until Isaac returned for her several months later.[17]

Then Barr continued on up to the colony. It was late Saturday night, May ninth, when he arrived.

The prairie dawn comes silently, a glow in the great eastern arch of the sky. The little knolls and hummocks cast a long blackness over the plains. As the sun eases over the rim the sky turns red and gold and little wracks of mist, all drawn and rosy, lie against the earth. Willow clumps spray upwards like red fingers, flushed with the urge of spring. The air is chill and bright.

His first morning on the site Isaac saw all this with pride. Near the big marquees the colonists slept in their little tents, a few dogs sniffed about where a wisp of smoke rose slow and straight above a burned-out fire.

These were his people—all British—and he had brought them here, five thousand miles, by ocean, rail and trail. For just a moment, as he raised the Red Ensign[18] over the sleeping camp he forgot his problems, his enormous fatigue, his frustrations and his loneliness. Before him, like a mirage, he saw the towns he had planned: Preston, Lloydtown and Barrview.

Gradually the camp awoke; in the chill morning there was a thin crackle of ice in the water pails. Isaac turned back to his tent.

Isaac Barr had been in trouble with some of his colonists from the moment the SS *Lake Manitoba* turned her nose toward Canada. Some of this arose from the fact there had been no real screening of those accepted as colonists. Applicants answered a questionnaire giving their names, occupations, marital status, capital, character references, farming experience; stating when they would be going to the colony, with the main party or later; travel preferences—cabin or third class; and whether, on reaching the colony, they intended to engage in business, hire out on a farm or take up a free-grant homestead.[19]

And so, for diverse reasons, they came. But despite warnings, they were not prepared for what they found: the discomforts of the voyage; the lack of amenities which they took for granted; the hardships of the trek from Saskatoon to Battleford.

They also resented the prices at Battleford and the colony site. Comparison of newspaper advertisements in the *Saskatchewan Herald,* Battleford's weekly paper at that time, shows no increase in prices after the colonists arrived, over what they were one month before.[20] But at the colony the prices had to be higher to cover the freighting costs.

Barr depended on the railroad. He depended on it to provide work for the colonists as well as to give access to the colony, to make it economically viable by providing a means of getting produce to the markets. When he was in Winnipeg in October of 1902 he had been assured by Mr. D. B. Hanna, third vice-president of the Canadian Northern Railway and by Mr. William Mackenzie, the president, that it would reach the colony in the summer of 1903.[21] Little did he know that at that time the railway was just a line on the map of the Territories and that Mackenzie and Mann had not even begun to raise the money needed to start construction.[22]

As always in his many dealings with officialdom, Barr was impressed. All his life he placed a naive trust in letterhead, title and office. But his colonists were less trusting.

All Mr. Barr's promises: Where were they now? The lumber for houses that was to have been on the site? And the sawmill? The lumber for two hundred houses had been ordered in Edmonton from McDougall and Secord[23] to be floated down the river to the landing at Fort Pitt just twenty miles north. But the ice had been longer in the North Saskatchewan than expected and the lumber had not been sent downstream. It was not there when the colonists expected it, ready to be nailed into houses. They blamed Barr.

One of the things that attracted colonists to the settlement was that they were to be near friends. When the section allotted to them was found to be unsuitable, marshy or too wooded for their liking they were indignant. Barr had misled them. Had he not claimed to have been all over the reservation? How they expected one man to know and be able to recall every acre in an area several hundred square miles is hard to understand. That they held it against him when he could not, is a measure of their insecurity and homesickness. Perhaps they forgot that he had repeated in his final pamphlet that they were free to exchange their location if, when they saw their homestead, they were dissatisfied.[24]

Some of the colonists had come with insufficient capital. With no work in sight and no crop for another year, with supplies so costly and the long winter ahead, they became timid and anxious. They wanted the money back they had invested in the stores syndicate or the hospital scheme. Barr had already suggested to them at Saskatoon that they take out in trade their investment in the store.[25]

Their dislike of Barr was a compound of his remoteness, lack of humour and authoritarian manner. His "Lambs" wanted a leader who would smooth the way and be a buffer against the strange and lonely land and their own fears and apprehensions. The fact that Barr wore a clerical collar reminded them that he was a priest, and he should do all this for them for priestly goodness, not for cash.

Their distrust of Barr was born of discomfort and apparently broken promises, from fears for their resources and the moneys they had invested. And since they already doubted Barr and his promises, they doubted his honesty. Although they had never seen him, many trusted him and were grateful for his efforts. But a minority turned against him when his arrangements failed and they felt threatened.

Harried by the colonists and harassed by their complaints, with plan after plan seeming to collapse, Barr reacted characteristically. After just four days in the colony he panicked and fled. Had he remained for another two weeks most of his troubles would have been over. The Barr Colony would have remained Barr's.

The Abdication

Barr simply got so crooked and people got so hostile that he thought he'd better get out of the country. He was really afraid of his hide. He thought he would get lynched, and no doubt he would have if they had caught him. One night he made up his mind to clear out, and he got his buckboard and a man that I knew quite well to drive him and they went out in the middle of the night. My wife was sick, back in a tent about twenty miles down the trail, and they heard Barr go by in the night. He was followed by a bunch of farmers in a wagon, with guns. And they stopped and asked my wife and her mother if they had seen Barr go by. And when they said no, they had been asleep, the farmers shouted, "Well, he's gone by here sometime in the night and we are after him and we are going to kill him!"[1]

Though many of the colonists will tell this story, and believe it too, it is not true.

I had decided to follow the Barr trail, but by car. For several days I had been talking with Barr Colonists in and around Lloydminster. There were not many left, and those still in the district were elderly and frail. Mrs. W. S. Topott, a spry eighty-five, had told me, "Coming out with the Barr Colony was a great experience." She had been in the last six weeks of her first pregnancy when they sailed from England. Her husband bought a hospital ticket on board ship and though they knew they would have to pay extra for her care they felt confident. While her husband went up to the site to locate his land, she had remained behind

92

on the trail, camped in their tent at the marquee beyond
Bresaylor. Here she went into labour. It was a tender tale,
the story of her delivery, of how the women made a straw
tick for her to lie on and how they sheltered her from the
cold. On the evening of the second day, May fifteenth, her
little son was born.

And then she told me that while she was in labour, the
day before the baby came, Barr had come by on his way
back from the colony wanting a change of horses. They had
given him a cup of tea, and when he heard that her baby
was to be born he gave her fifty cents as a gift for the child.
"I often wish I had kept it, but in those days fifty cents was
quite a bit of money."²

A few days later as I sped past Paynton, a hamlet near
Bresaylor, I noticed an old log barn on the outskirts of the
tiny town. I wondered, could it have belonged to Peter
Paynter, that retired policeman who had farmed near here
and helped so many of the colonists? So I turned aside and
sought the local postmaster. It wasn't Paynter's. But if I
was interested in the old times the man next door to the
post office remembered a lot. And so I met Mr. Dobie. "The
man you want to see is Lachlan Taylor," he said. "He knew
Jack Barr. Of course if he doesn't like you he won't talk to
you." And he led me across the street to a prairie shack.

Lachlan was an enormous man. He was seated in a great
armchair in one corner of the main room. He seemed about
eighty years old and looked to be part Indian. For several
minutes he just stared at me saying nothing as I asked him
if he remembered the Barrs. In the dim light I became
aware that in the opposite corner an Indian woman rocked
silently. If she understood what was said she gave no sign.

That day Lachlan talked. Barr had hired him in Saskatoon to go up to the colony site and locate the place it was
to be and put up a tent for the stores. Barr supplied him
with a democrat, team and driver. He located the survey,
put up the tent and stayed about ten days, and was on his
way back to Saskatoon when he met Barr, the two doctors
and the nurses coming up. They had the storekeeper with
them to set up the stores. So far the timing and the persons

involved checked with what I knew. Barr then sent Taylor up to Onion Lake, the Indian reservation just north of the colony site, to buy lumber, meat and provisions for the stores. When he got back Isaac Barr was ready to pull out; to leave the colony. The memory of the aged is a fickle thing but I knew I was hearing fact, for in the University of Saskatchewan Archives is a letter from the Indian agent at Onion Lake, handed to "Mr. Taylor who intends leaving in the morning," to return to headquarters camp to report to Barr. The letter, dated May twelfth, stated what supplies the agent had available. It was the buying trip Lachlan had referred to. The date was right.

"Like I said, when I got back from Onion Lake there was Reverend Barr ready to pull out. We decided to go down together. We both took democrats. We left Lloydminster just at early daybreak. Had dinner at Blue Hill. Drove to Bresaylor the first day and Battleford the next. Barr stayed at the Albion Hotel." And then Lachlan told me how they had stopped along the way at a place where a lady was going to have a baby. And "Barr gave her fifty cents as a present for the kid."[3]

The myth of the midnight escape had vanished! Mrs. Topott knew her baby's birthday. Both she and Lachlan told the story of the fifty cents and yet they had never seen one another nor talked together.

Lloyd arrived at Battleford the evening of May fourteenth or fifteenth from Saskatoon, "in a gale of stinging sleet or snow."[4] This is odd since the meteorological bureau reports the high and low at Battleford for those two days were eighty-three and fifty-eight, sixty-seven and fifty degrees.[5] He was met, he said, by worried and excited colonists. Some had been to the colony site and had found Barr's prices excessive, others claimed that Barr had bought up all the oats at Peter Paynter's place at twenty-five cents a bushel and was charging them a dollar-fifty. Many had found the prairie blackened by grass fires (likely set by the colonists themselves) and imagined that the land was ruined. Some were on their way back and others were too upset by the reports to take the trail themselves.

Barr "fleeing" the camp arrived on the evening of the fifteenth.[6] It was to be a confrontation of the two priests.

Lloyd wrote that he called a meeting of the colonists still in Battleford for 2 p.m. the following day. One hundred and forty attended (about seven per cent). In his address ". . . he reviewed the deplorable condition of the colonists" (he had not yet been up to the site himself) and said it was time for immediate action to "take the bull by the horns and place the colony on a proper business footing." He "regretted the change that had come over Barr."

After much talk Nathaniel Jones moved a resolution that "they no longer look to I. M. Barr as leader, and that the name Barr should no longer be applied to them in the British Colony." This was passed unanimously. "Then came the suggestion that I should be made Director of the British Colony. This I objected to [Lloyd was already employed as chaplain by the Colonial and Continental Church Society]. But, it was urged, if I sent the society the unanimous resolution of that mass meeting the church would surely be willing to help them out of their difficulty. This I agreed to do, on condition that a committee of 12 should be elected, some immediately and some when the settlement was completed. Mr. Blackburn, Mr. Still and Mr. Nathaniel Jones were the first three elected."[7]

These were the men who confronted Barr at the hotel that evening. They had employed the intervening hours consulting the commander of the local detachment of the mounted police. He decided that the police could take no criminal action at law against Barr; only civil action could be taken by the colonists. Undaunted by the fact that the police did not see Barr as a criminal, Lloyd, Jones and Still pressed their demands. Government Agent Speers and several others were with Barr.

BARR DEPOSED AS LEADER! say the newspaper headlines of the times.[8] Deposed is a ludicrous word for the sorry little scene acted out in the hotel that night. How could he be

deposed by a committee of colonists? They had not elected
nor appointed him leader. They could not fire him from the
companies he had formed, since none of those present was
on the board of directors of those companies. The idea, the
organization, the arrangements, all the work and all the
original capital were Barr's. They were in no way bound to
serve him. He had not been set over them by an authority.
They were free to act as they chose. Deposed? Nonsense!
Barr abdicated.

Nathaniel Jones read him the resolution passed by the
meeting, and "Mr. Barr opened with a tirade against the
colonists . . . they were a crowd of ruffians . . . they had
threatened his life . . . he could not go up to the colony
without a police escort," said Lloyd in retrospect. Lloyd
pointed out that if what Barr said was true he had lost the
confidence of the colonists and the only thing left to do was
to sign the agreement: to abdicate. "Mr. Speers took an
active part in the discussions and seemed to be more anxious
to let I. M. Barr out than to help the committee carry on."[9]
The government agent supported Barr.[10] Lloyd could not
forgive Speers for standing up for Barr. Three years later,
in a letter to Professor Mavor dated March 23, 1906, he
wrote: "Most of the information you received came directly
from Mr. Speers. Naturally you assumed that a government
agent in his position should be absolutely reliable. Unfortunately that is not the case. Wilfully or not, I cannot say
but he has always been down on anything English."

A more dynamic, forceful man than Barr would have
thrown them out. Now that things were beginning to work,
now that the people, the stores and the hospital were on
the colony site, now that the delays and deficiencies were
almost over, why should he give up? Why should he hand
over his dreams to Lloyd, Still and Jones?

The answer lay in Isaac's character. He never could face
a row. As a child he had learned to avoid his father's mighty
wrath. As an adult, "He was a peace-loving man who
backed away from a confrontation; a gentle type of man
who would go out of his way to avoid a quarrel. He could

not take criticism."[11] It was easier to give up. And so he signed the little agreements they placed before him. His capitulation was ignominious and complete.

He resigned all claim to his homestead. This was to have been the town site for Barrview. "We have given Mr. Barr $800.00 in recognition of what we call a 'moral obligation' in the matter of the homestead for which he intended to enter. This goes towards his [just] debts," Lloyd explained to the Deputy Minister of the Interior.[12] What just debts? And who decided they were so? Thas was a paper credit; the committee had no money. I will let Lloyd relate what happened to Barr's homestead:

We were all camped on the school section and everybody knew quite well that we could not stay there. After I returned from the Barr Conference Fiasco and reported that he had gone to parts unknown, I went to . . . the Government Agent for land, in the colony and found that I. M. Barr and *others of his intimate group** had their names down for the four quarters of the section immediately south of the school section. [The agent] agreed at once to wipe those names off and put on the four names I gave him instead, my own being on the southwest quarter. I don't think he knew at the time what I had in mind . . . [Lloyd intended to give this property for the new town site.] I knew the three holders of the other quarter-sections, with me, were quite willing to turn over their holdings with mine (my Lay Reader . . . was one of them).[13]

Thus it was Barr's homestead Lloyd so generously donated later! And did he recompense "the members of Barr's intimate group" who also lost the homesteads they had chosen?

Barr also resigned all claim to any other homestead in the colony. This was grovelling! Barr was a free citizen and entitled to take up a homestead anywhere in Canada that he chose.

He signed over all the stores then on the ground to satisfy the claims of shareholders. An inventory showed them to

---

*Italics supplied.

be worth at least two thousand dollars. Many of the colonists had taken out their shares in trade as Barr had urged in the last pamphlet. There must have been some losses. Due to haste and lack of permanent buildings, goods had been carelessly handled both at Saskatoon and the camp site. It was difficult to keep stock safe in a tent. "Some colonists just took things from the store. They justified this by saying they were entitled to the goods, it was really theirs, they owned stock in the stores."[14] Barr offered to buy back outstanding shares at twenty-one dollars for a twenty-five dollar share but the colonists wanted $22.50.[15] It is remarkable that, though many accounts say the stores syndicate was defunct, Lloyd was still able to sell to those on the site the shares of those who had not come up to the colony but had remained in other parts of Canada and wanted their money out.

Barr also signed over all the hospital equipment to satisfy medical staff and contract ticket holders. The terms read:

"In consideration of the sum of £350, more or less, received by me from members of the British Colony Hospital for contract tickets, I hereby agree to hand over to the Rev. G. E. Lloyd and the Committee all the hospital supplies, medicines, surgical instruments, hospital furniture and all other hospital equipment, whether at Saskatoon, on the trail, at Headquarters Camp, the said Rev. G. E. Lloyd and the Committee undertaking to discharge all claims on Mr. Barr in respect to the hospital to the value of the stores received.

Witness: J. F. D. Parker   *Signed*: I. M. Barr[16]
         M. S. Griffin

As Lloyd told the story, Barr assured him the supplies were in a box marked with a red cross in the marquee at the camp site. (All the supplies in one box?) When this was opened it was found to contain nothing but a broken cot and a mattress. "Then we heard he [Barr] had sold everything up and down the railway line and had skipped across the line to the States."[17]

The story of what they found in the box may be true. The total capitalization of the hospital was less than two thousand dollars, and Barr had employed and transported two nurses from England. True, he had not paid salaries to the doctors but a tent hospital had been in operation for a month in Saskatoon and a week or so at the colony site. The tent itself remained. It must have cost a considerable sum as an active hospital and, considering the number of sick whom Lloyd had stayed behind in Saskatoon to comfort, the supplies would be considerably depleted.

As a last act of abdication Isaac turned over his books to Lloyd, a terrible blunder, for thereafter Lloyd refused him access to them.[18] Barr's secretary, George Flamank, followed the books to the service of Lloyd and the committee.

Defeat, so close to success, must have been a crushing thing for Isaac. Exhausted, rejected, maligned, ashamed of his capitulation, he had no one to turn to in his distress. Christina, who had shared his dream, was far away. Those colonists still his followers were scattered over the colony reservation, too busy with the realities of survival in what seemed to them a harsh land to be aware of what had happened to him, too busy to come to his support.

But Barr had not skipped across the line to the States. On the contrary, for the next three weeks he was encamped two miles from Battleford, available to all the colonists to settle up accounts.[19] He offered to refund the fifteen hundred dollars he had received for absentee fees, but without access to the books how could he?

There was real confusion about the homestead entries that had been paid for because of Lloyd's persistent refusal to let Barr check them against the books. In spite of this no colonist suffered loss. Barr still had an account with the Canadian government and all the claims against it were paid.

The figures appear in the Dominion Archives in Ottawa, File 758120, Reference 12370, Report from the Auditor General to Deputy Minister of the Interior:

Balance on hand December 31, 1903			$2,759.65
Refunds granted since			
Names not on list	21 @ $10	$210	
Entries granted since			
Names not on list	22 @ $10	$220	
		$430	$2,329.65
Refund Bank of Montreal			1,500.00*
Balance			829.65

There are 20 applications for refunds whose names are not on the lists but who have not forwarded Barr's receipts. If we deduct $200 for these

Balance $629.65

Statement January 6, 1904.

The refunds were paid, with or without the lists!

By September 16, 1904, the balance was $679.65 and on December 20, 1904, it stood at $459.65.[20]

Here the file closed. These were the homestead entries, and care had been taken to account for those who could not produce receipts. At three per cent interest compounded annually, what amount now stands to Barr's credit with the government of Canada?

I have tried without success to find a colonist who himself lost money to Barr or knew someone who did. "The men of substance were too astute to give anyone money. And the others never had much to give."[21] Mrs. Topott told me she lost her hospital ticket fee, and I am sure most of the three hundred or so who bought tickets did lose their five dollars. The idea was a good one, it attracted a doctor and nurses who remained with the colony, but medicare is expensive and the price of the tickets was unrealistic even for those times.

---

*This represents the refund to W. T. R. Preston.

Did Barr make money out of his colony scheme? No. He lost what little he had. He spent his own modest means to publish his pamphlets. He paid the Dominion government five thousand dollars and got Mr. W. T. R. Preston, the Canadian government emigration agent in London, to put up twenty-five hundred dollars for him to secure the reservation for the colony site. This he hoped to repay from the bonuses he expected from the government.[22, 23]

For a con man, a "bester," a man on the make, the following is certainly out of character:

To James A. Smart Esq.,
Deputy Minister of the Interior,
Ottawa.

August 31, 1903

DEAR SIR,

In connection with the payment of £ 1,500 made by me to you in London as homestead entry fees on homesteads to be taken up by members of my party, I wish to advise you that of this amount Mr. W. T. R. Preston has secured £ 500 in view of the fact that I was not able to deposit more than £ 1,000 myself in order to have the lands reserved. As I am no longer connected with the organization of this colony and am not bringing out any further number of immigrants to locate in the district, and consequently have no further interest in the reservation, I would ask you to kindly accept this as an order to pay the Manager of the Bank of Montreal, London, England £ 500 of any balance due me in connection with this payment, to recoup the amount which Mr. Preston secured for me. I understand there will be from £ 900 to £ 1,000 remaining in the hands of the government for which entry fees will not be asked, and the amount can be paid out of such balance.

Yours truly,
I. M. Barr[24]

Though the colonists felt a priest should work for the love of mankind, not for money, Barr was not in the business for philanthropy. Perhaps he did not make this clear. Certainly he asked them no fee for his services and as a result he had no working capital. The steamship company paid him thirteen thousand dollars' commission and threw in the trip by ship and rail to the Canadian West to choose the location. Eight thousand dollars of this he spent on his London office, in "clerk hire, postage, printing, rent and other expenses."

"Mr. Barr had an office in London which I am satisfied from what I saw of it would cost the whole amount he received in steamship bonuses. He had a large office, employed a large staff, did much advertising."[25]

He lost money on horses, the carload smothered on the way to Saskatoon; a large part of the first consignment of tents was stolen; only two hundred of the five hundred groundsheets he ordered and paid for ever arrived; not all the stoves he purchased for the colonists were sold, because of late delivery. His total losses on the scheme were ten thousand dollars, he claimed, though this was probably an exaggeration.

If he made any money, the course of his later life gave no evidence of it. In a statement given before Lord Tennyson's Committee concerning "Agricultural Settlements in the British Colonies," James A. Smart stated that the Canadian government had paid Barr nothing and, in direct response to a question whether there had been any deception of the colonists by Barr, replied, "Well, I do not know where the deception came in. There is no deception as far as we know."[26]

As part of the immigration policy of the Laurier government, the Deputy Minister of the Interior willingly undertook to make both the trip to the colony site and the establishment of the settlement as attractive as possible. The government provided two experienced farmers from the area to give lectures to the colonists at Saskatoon on the conditions they would meet and to advise them what equipment to buy first, and how to arrange for further purchases. These two men, Dale and Snow, travelled up to the colony as did Herbert Hall, the agriculturalist engaged by Lloyd.[27] The government "willingly" provided the large wayside marquees and the stoves and wood with which they were equipped. All this had been arranged with the department before the colonists arrived. The CPR and the government also provided transport to the colony, or so the Deputy Minister testified.[28] Let P. G. Laurie, of the *Saskatchewan Herald*, Battleford, rail against Barr! These things were provided not as a last-minute stop-gap by immigration officers, but by previous arrangement with the Immigration Department, as his own paper records. [29,30]

Transportation was available, though it was not provided by Barr himself.[31] Local farmers and Indians from the nearby reservations supplemented the government and railroad services by picking up what loads they could get.

Before he closed his testimony, Mr. Smart said he could find nothing definite about overcharging by Barr. When he was asked, "Didn't all the [Saskatoon] storekeepers swear that Barr asked a commission from them?" he replied, "Not at all. I think those which did not get the business raised the cry."[32]

Mr. Smart was not alone in his opinion:

Although the colonists were settling 160 miles to the west, Saskatoon regarded them as her customers. While the colonists were encamped at Saskatoon the "Phenix" was much incensed at a mail order house distributing catalogues.* The following year the "Phenix" made much ado when it was rumoured that the Barr Colonists intended to open a route to Edmonton. Several articles appeared dealing with "the perils and almost impassable stretches of country" between Lloydminster and Edmonton.[33]

This was the tough West and even Lloyd at times was out of his depth. On shipboard Barr told him he had made a contract with Mr. Secord of Edmonton for two thousand

*A mail order house flooded the district with catalogues and added insult to injury by erecting a billboard—Saskatoon's first. Later the local council talked of pulling it down, claiming that it frightened horses.

bushels of potatoes at a cost of two thousand dollars, to be floated down the river to Hewitt's Landing just north of the colony. A wise move, Lloyd agreed, for they would provide food and seed. But the scow arrived at the landing just after Barr had departed the colony and *Mr. Secord* decided to send it on with the flood tide to Battleford. The mistake, the misjudgment, the breach of contract were all Mr. Secord's. Barr refused to pay for the potatoes when Secord turned up at his hotel in Battleford demanding money. Lloyd was not so astute. He and his committee took over the contract and borrowed money to pay Mr. Secord for his own mistake. Lloyd commented, "And had Barr acted at all fairly it might have been a help instead of the total loss it became."[34] Yes, this was the tough West, and the chaplain had a lot to learn about business too.

Had Barr remained with the colony another few weeks his success would have been certain. Within two weeks, far from disposing of the store, Nathaniel Jones was operating it.[35] John Barr had taken over the transport service and several colonists had become freighters. The headquarters camp had a restaurant.

There was an old Dutch lady, Miss Posthuma, came out with the colony. She was rather corpulent, with a pair of big gold-rimmed glasses, and red hair straggling all over her face. She was a fine old soul and a real good cook. She could see where there was a chance of opening a restaurant to feed those people if she could get enough food.

Mr. Lloyd wouldn't be pleased but there was nothing to do on Sunday so we hit on the idea of riding the steers down in the corral waiting to be sold. We'd put a saddle on one of the wild steers and run a crupper under his tail, and then draw straws for who would ride him. It came to be my lot one Sunday morning. They blindfolded the steer till I got on then let him go. Well, he headed up the alleyway between the tents until he came to the open door of Miss Posthuma's restaurant tent all set up with tables and cutlery and all like that. She looked up and she saw this steer with a man on his back coming through the door. She let out a yell and headed for the rear exit screaming, and the steer after her with half the tent trailing on his horns. He unloaded me as he headed out to the open prairie. We had to take up a collection to pay for the tent being fixed up, but what fun! Mr. Lloyd took a dim view of it all. Perhaps because it was Sunday.

Then old Mrs. Salmon started a restaurant too. She didn't know a rooster from a hen. The boys got hold of a rooster she had bought and they told her this rooster would hatch eggs for her. So they got an old box and they cut a couple of holes in it, put the rooster's legs through the holes. Then they put some eggs under him in the box and tied him in. There he was for the next three days walking around the camp with the box on his back. He wasn't a very good hatcher.[36]

"Mrs. Salmon had a husband, Mr. Salmon, but she also had Mr. Ramsbottom too!"[37]

Lumber was brought down from Onion Lake and rafts were floated down the Saskatchewan River from Edmonton to Hewitt's Landing and Fort Pitt, bringing supplies for the store and some farm equipment. The rafts were then broken up for lumber. It was all just as Barr had promised.

On July twenty-first Lloyd, in a letter addressed to all the colonists, made the abdication final. After stating how busy he had been trailing Barr about trying to straighten up the mess the former "Leader" had left, he started off: "The British Colony is not dead, and the members of the British Colony now living in . . . the first reservation desire that the name Barr shall no longer be applied to them." He continued with a list of railway and government officials they should contact about various problems and closed with: "By a unanimous vote in three places it was decided the name of the whole twenty-odd townships should be Britannia, N.W.T., and the name of the first town Lloydminster. This address has been sent to the postal authorities and is now official. . . ."[38]

For the women, the loneliness and the isolation, the cold and the life without comforts were especially hard:

It just broke my mother's heart. She brought her sewing machine out, she had been used to her children having the best of clothes. The few clothes she brought out were not suitable for the weather. I can always remember how humiliated I was to have the seat of my trousers patched with a piece of flour sack and it said "Five Roses." Father was very leary about spending his capital and there was no income coming in for years and there were no comforts, no refinements. We had nothing in the home. All my life I slept on a wooden box. I never slept in a bed until after I left home. The first bed I ever slept in was in a hospital.[39]

A telegraph line strung between the colony and Battleford ended some of the feeling of isolation.

Dominion Day that year, 1903, was celebrated with horse-racing and prizes and that night there was a concert: all this just seven weeks after Barr's abdication.[40] Within the year there were a rifle range, tennis courts and an operatic society.

Lloyd's committee meetings had petered out. Who needed them? "There is some that stay around Lloydminster that do nothing but call public meetings, but they are not working colony."[41]

"A few gregarious spirits for a time fluttered around the altar candles revelling in the rituals and ceremonies of the inner office shrine and basking in the fierce white light shed by the new leader. The sycophants, the satellites, the rump administrators hung around the headquarters camp for a few months then vanished—some very slowly like smoke on a calm evening, others swiftly like jets of steam in a high wind."[42]

By October, just six months after the arrival in Saint John, Lloydminster had two large stores, a post office, a telegraph office, a drugstore, a saddlery, and a harness shop, two butcher shops, a blacksmith's shop, a carpenter's shop, three restaurants, a livery stable, seventy-five houses, but no liquor licence."[43]

Lloyd's views on liquor were well known:

I remember Lloyd having some very sharp words . . . over
the question of having a licensed hotel or bar in the village.
He was not at all in favour of anyone being able to buy alco-
holic beverages. He wanted the whole colony to be absolutely dry.
    We liked Mr. Lloyd very, very much but he was a dictator
with very strong ideas. He was under the impression that
progress was linked entirely with his church.
    Of course Lloyd wouldn't co-operate with anybody. You
had to co-operate with Lloyd. He was above Barr, you
understand, he was a representative of God. Mr. Barr was
just merely the organizer of the whole scheme.
    Mr. Barr made it plain that he did not want to be clergy-
man of the colony. He just wanted to get things organized
and started. Let Lloyd look after their souls, he would look
after their bodies. And of course Mr. Barr would take a
drink. In those days it was considered that you weren't
much of a man if you wouldn't. But we never knew of him
to be drunken.[44]

In the opinion of another colonist,

Mr. Lloyd, being the clergyman, was very anxious to get the
church started. He seemed to think religious teaching was
more important than something to eat. He fussed about the
church. Got the logs cut by the Indians up at Onion Lake
through another clergyman. We used to call him "Old Lying
Jack Matheson." He's dead now so he won't hear me. We
hauled the logs down and some of the original settlers paid
five dollars a log and had their names embedded each in his
own log. This was the first church.[45]

    Two years later a local policeman wrote to Professor
Mavor: "The Reverend Lloyd has happily for all concerned
been promoted or translated, or whatever is the correct
ecclesiastical term and will shortly go away. I often think
he lived some centuries too late; what a glorious Inquisitor
he would have made!"[46]
    Lloyd left to become Archdeacon of Saskatchewan and
later Bishop.

But Lloyd had not finished with Barr yet. In his memoirs, published in 1940 three years after Barr's death, the bishop destroyed the man.

In fairness, I should mention that when these memoirs were written Bishop Lloyd was seventy-nine years old and in failing health. He was describing events that had occurred half a lifetime earlier. Therefore the very few errors of fact such as dates, locations and so forth will be ignored; only those things will be considered which condemn Isaac Barr either by outright statement or by innuendo. Barr was dead and one cannot libel the dead. In *The Trail of 1903* the Right Reverend George Exton Lloyd administered the final blow to leave Isaac Montgomery Barr "all silent and all damned." There is not a single word of praise or kindness in the entire manuscript.

"The Boer War had come to an end and England was flooded with disbanded soldiers," wrote Lloyd. "All over the country people were talking emigration . . . so I wrote a letter to the London *Times* suggesting that as I had been twenty years in Canada I might be able to advise some of those who were thinking of going out . . . An I. M. Barr," a clergyman doing summer duty at St. Saviour's Church, Tollington Park, asked for a meeting with Lloyd saying he was organizing a colony to go to the Northwest. He told Lloyd he was a graduate of Western College, Ontario, and as a student had taken summer duty in a church in Windsor with Canon Hurst, who was then Lloyd's superior in London. Canon Hurst recalled little of the student beyond the fact that he was satisfactory, and Lloyd turned over to Barr the letters he had received with enquiries about Canada.

In doing this I made the same mistake which I suppose the rector of St. Saviour's Tollington Park made. He should have applied to the Archbishop of Canterbury to see whether I. M. Barr's credentials were alright, because no clergyman is allowed to take duty in any church in England without licence from the Archbishop, and that is only issued on letters from the Diocesan Bishop of the clergyman applying.

I took it for granted the rector had seen the licence and as he was away on holiday I could not consult him. What little I could find out from Canon Hurst satisfied me and I turned over to him [Barr] everything I had, thinking my part in this emigration movement was now ended.[47]

If Lloyd really had these doubts he himself could have enquired from the Archbishop of Canterbury, and he would have seen both the licence and the letter.[48] But now, thirty-seven years after the event, he could safely suggest that they did not exist; he could imply that Barr was representing himself as something he was not.

His Lordship went on to describe how Barr was careless with money.

Whenever I had opportunity I looked in to the office Mr. Barr had established in Seargent's [sic] Inn and I sometimes suggested changes. For instance he had engaged Mr. Flamank as secretary and he was worried and nervous at the rush of business. Money was coming in for store shares, medical shares, blankets and tents, C.P.R. lands and $10 homestead fees, and Mr. Barr would stuff the money into all his pockets before going home for the night. I suggested he might be knocked down by a cab—he might be waylaid by somebody who had come into the office, or he might be taken ill with all that money in his possession. He listened to the extent that he asked the Canadian Government offices to send up a clerk every morning to take over all the homestead fees and any other government money. So that was alright. Then I suggested that he ought to have an escort home each evening . . . and as far as I know he did it. But it was not my business and I did not feel justified in making too many suggestions. Although he was *under obligation** to me.

It is the phrases "he would stuff all the money into all his pockets" and "under obligation to me" that are deadly. (In truth, Lloyd understated his role; he did more than drop in occasionally. He had been in charge of the colony business when Barr was in Canada in October selecting the colony site.)

"The Ottawa people said they had paid him [Barr]

---
*Italics supplied.

nothing by way of immigration capitation grant [neither they had] because of the expense they had been put to for marquees and stoves every twenty miles along the trail. That may be so, but—"

This is precisely how Lloyd closed the chapter. But what? Or consider: "We at once took possession of what stores were left in the marquee belonging to the shareholders of the I. M. Barr co-operative store project, and took a detailed inventory of what there was there. But we found little of actual food left. There were things of the slow-selling variety—pitchforks, axle grease, knapsacks, a few tin articles, but not much else."⁴⁹ Just two-thousand-dollars' worth else!

But Lloyd was nearing the end of his memoirs. He had to finish Barr off: "Mr. Smart told me he had found out all about I. M. Barr's record and why he originally left the diocese of Saskatchewan. The government would have stopped the whole expedition if they had known earlier, but it was too late, the SS *Lake Manitoba* was on the way. . . . I asked him why they did not give me some sort of hint of what they knew and he replied that they were afraid I was of the same ilk."⁵⁰ There is only the innuendo. What had Smart found out? Whatever it was, he failed to mention it to Lord Tennyson's Committee. *Ilk?* Then, drawing his priestly garb about him, Lloyd resumed: " 'Well,' I said, 'You had only to ask in Toronto. I was a graduate of Wycliffe College in 1885 and was a member of the University Company and chaplain of the first regiment in Canada, the Queen's Own, for five years.' " Ten days after the publication of these memoirs Bishop Lloyd was dead.

For nearly forty years he had nourished his hatred of Barr, a composite of envy of the dreamer, abhorrence of all drinking and a missionary zeal that could not tolerate a man who disavowed church doctrine (Lloyd must have discovered this) but continued to wear a clerical collar.

Some of Lloyd's bitterness about Barr may have resulted from the incident of the horses. When, on the last day on shipboard the Lloyds had received the presentation of three hundred dollars from the colonists toward the purchase of a buckboard and a pair of horses when they should arrive at Saskatoon, "[Barr] said he had arranged for a number of horses to be on sale at Saskatoon and on his promise to see we got a good choice the committee turned over the $300 to him. . . ."

At Saskatoon Lloyd chose his horses:

We selected the two largest that were left, though they were not well matched—the one old and steady and the other younger and skittish. . . . The price was $500. I paid down $200 in cash and told Jack Barr that I. M. Barr had the $300 of the testimonial. . . . Jack Barr said that would be quite alright but they were running "the Horses" as a separate affair from I. M. Barr. . . . If I would give him a note of hand for the $300 he would cash that with I. M. Barr and that would keep both accounts straight. So I gave him the note for the $300 and took the horses.

I left my horses and wagon with my family at Battleford while I was going through the troubles with I. M. Barr at the Queen's Hotel. . . . At one time I spoke to him about that $300 note and he said he had it and would give it to me when he could get at his papers. [Could Barr have been bargaining here: Give me access to my books and I'll give you the note?] In the pressure of events I forgot about the note for after all the three suggested agreements with I. M. Barr came to an untimely end by his clearing off for the U.S.A. . . . .

Exactly three months after leaving Battleford I received a demand from the Union Bank in Saskatoon for $300 and interest due them on a note . . . they said it was my note alright and it had been negotiated by I. M. Barr . . . they had cashed it in good faith and therefore according to law, I must accept responsibility for it as I. M. Barr could not be reached.[51]

Obviously Jack Barr had presented the note to Isaac. Isaac gave him three hundred dollars, then later cashed the note at the bank. This was a fraudulent use of the note. Why Isaac used it in this way may have been partly his hatred of

Lloyd and partly an attempt to recoup some of the money
he claimed to have advanced for Lloyd's passage to Canada.[52] For either reason it was inexcusable.

Lloyd immediately followed this account with a detailed
and unnecessary story of Jack Barr, obviously suggested to
him, as he stated in the first sentence, by his distress over the
matter of the note:

What little I know of the end of Jack Barr may be of interest
to the colonists, although I don't think he was responsible
for what happened to my note. I was typing the correspondence as Archdeacon of Saskatchewan, on the sleeping car
of the Canadian National Railway when my wife called my
attention to a commotion at the other end of the car, and
said, "That looks like Jack Barr." I went down the car and
found he was holding up the passengers demanding to see
their tickets, etc. Without much trouble he was persuaded
to go back to his own people in the forward car. A little
later the same thing happened again, and again I went
down the car but it was not so easy this time. I said,"Do you
know me?" He looked at me for a moment and then said,
"Yes, you are Mr. Lloyd." I said, "You must leave these
people alone and go back to your own people." He had
been to the exhibition in Saskatoon and, whether brought
on by drinking I could not say, but it was evidently now
something more serious than that. I edged him back to his
own people and a railway man came up and took charge of
him. Evidently the conductor telegraphed ahead to Battleford and an ambulance was waiting to take him to the
Mental Hospital. I heard afterwards that he died there.[53]

In spite of Lloyd's assertion that Barr had skipped out of
the country he was still in the area. June thirteenth, four
weeks after the abdication, he was still in Battleford or had
just left that day,[54] and on July seventh he was still in Saskatoon.[55] On July fifteenth he asked the Dominion government in Ottawa for the capitation fee to which he believed
himself entitled. His request was refused.[56]

In the Dominion Archives is a letter dated October 15,
1903, from P.O. Box 589, Toronto. It is addressed to a government official and says: "Several people have written me

complaining that I have not sent them receipts for homestead fees which they claim to have remitted. If this is the
case I am very sorry for it. The fault lies with my secretary
Mr. Flamank now in the employ of the Committee of the
All British Colony Settlement. If they can establish their
claims I shall be glad if the amounts can be refunded out
of the deposit of £1,500 I made with the Deputy Minister
of the Interior.

I shall always be glad to render what help I can and to set
matters right in this or any other respect. No one regrets
more than I the unfortunate turn affairs took.

Sincerely, I. M. Barr[57]

But Barr was supposed to have vanished. How would the
"several people" know where to address him? And with no
access to the books, the ruling imposed by Lloyd, how could
he send them receipts?

Though Lloyd wrote freely about Barr, only once did
Barr publicly express an opinion of Lloyd. In Pamphlet
Number Two, addressed to the colonists, Barr had said:

I desire to acknowledge the valuable services which [Lloyd]
has rendered in the promotion of this colonizing project
(both by voice and by pen). . . . During my absence from
England he had charge of the movement. . . . Mr. Lloyd's
intimate knowledge of the country where we are to settle
and his practical grasp of affairs will prove valuable factors
in the success of the colony. In him I have found an intelli-
gent and congenial co-adjutor. I predict a high position for
Mr. Lloyd in Church councils in Canada. . . . I should add
that Mr. Lloyd won his laurels at Battleford in the Rebellion
of 1885. As a member of the Queen's Own of Toronto Canada he distinguished himself by exceptional bravery and
gallantry, and was recommended for the Victoria Cross
which he would have obtained had he been in the regular
army. Mr. Lloyd is a modest man and seldom speaks of these
matters.[58]

Just after the abdication, in interviews with the press, he
declined to criticize Lloyd or any individual colonist. "Mr.
Barr is certain of the colony's success and thinks they will do

well and become prosperous. Mr. Lloyd who is practically the leader of the colony continues very popular and Mr. Barr considers they are getting on very satisfactorily." He went on to discuss the reasons for the problems that arose. The only mention he made of Lloyd was to say, "Every day I had to open hundreds of letters personally and one day they reached 1,100 so you can see how the work rushed on me. I had practically no help. Rev. Mr. Lloyd was only the chaplain and did not undertake any of the detail work, luckily perhaps, so that all complaints were directed to me for explanation. I had the entire responsibility of the undertaking both financially and as to its management."[59]

But Barr had his own thoughts about Lloyd. In later years he referred to him in the privacy of his own family as "that snivelling little parson who came to me pleading to be taken along so I paid his passage and gave him money to buy clothes for his wife."[60]

Just when Barr and Christina were reunited I do not know. "When the colony business was finished up, he came and got Christina and they went away."[61]

He never returned to Canada, though he always referred to it in later years with affection and a degree of yearning.[62]

The Bitter Years

The bitter years had begun for Isaac. He lived daily with the knowledge that when the success of his great venture lay just over the prairie horizon he had failed, he had given up, intimidated by a few colonists and a priest so bigoted that he could see the colony only as an extension of his missionary effort; so rigid in his rectitude that he could see the empire-building visionary only as a force which must ultimately be purged from the colony and forgotten.

Barr had hoped to make money from the scheme; instead it left him poor. "His philosophy was that of a businessman. The one that was doing all the work should be paid. He mentioned that many times. He was a businessman and the mere fact that he was also a priest had nothing to do with it."[1]

The bitter years had begun for Christina too. Who was she? Christina Helberg was just twenty-one years old when she went to work as a clerk-typist for Isaac Barr in his London office early in January, 1903. At that time a young lady usually remained at home until some man took over her support by marrying her. But the Helbergs were German immigrants to England. Christian, her father, worked as a barman[2] and his daughter had to work too.

Dark-haired and with rather close-set eyes, she was not beautiful in a classical sense. Besides she had a slightly receding chin. But her youth, vivacity and gaiety attracted Isaac, already thrice married and thirty-five years older than she was.

When she began to work for him, his plans for filling the western territories with people were already well advanced. Would-be settlers applied by the hundreds to join Barr's colony, the money for homestead reservations flowed in; the railway had been promised; steamship and rail transportation, banking, stores, hospital, the chaplain, all were arranged. His dreaming was unfettered. In the flush of these early successes and in the sense of power he felt, he loved Christina.

When the office closed for the day he would take her to dinner and the theatre, to the musicals; for her it was a world of enchantment and excitement.[3] As he talked on about the colony: Canada for the British; the Canadian Co-operative; the far-off land of the prairie sunrise; the rich, rich wheatland; Barrview, his community and his place in it, he was another Rhodes building an empire. And as she listened she tasted the wine of his dreaming.

Christina sailed cabin class on the SS *Lake Manitoba*.[4] Her parents probably opposed her going. The distance and the dictates of lower-middle-class morality must have concerned them, but she was of age, it was a job and, after all, Isaac was a priest. I do not know precisely when he gave her the ring. If it was before he left England this may have reassured Christian and Johanna Helberg. Simple and beautiful in design, it has three long opals set side by side and surrounded by small diamonds.[5]

Isaac offered much more than himself—adventure, status as the wife of the colony leader, property—so that Christina forgot that he was more than old enough to be her father; that by the time she was just thirty-five and still young, he would have lived his three score years and ten.

They saw little of each other during the voyage for there was no privacy on the overcrowded ship. All day and far into the night Isaac was in his cabin, busy with colony business. They may have had a few hours together in Saint John but Christina left with the other colonists while Isaac went by regular service to Ottawa.

Had Christina been with him at Battleford when he was confronted by Lloyd and the other colonists, I am not sure he would have abdicated. She was young and strong and determined. All she expected from this venture was at risk. Young though she was, she was too disciplined to retreat. But she was not with Isaac; she was nearly two thousand miles away in Markham,[6] and there was only the impersonal long-distance telegraph for communication.

Not that she would be unaware of all that was going on. The Toronto papers, without exception, carried the story in detail: ALL-BRITISH COLONY COMES TO IGNOMINIOUS END. PRO-MOTER HAS RETURNED CASH AND SETTLERS ARE SCATTERED.[7] MR. BARR DEPOSED. MEETING OF COLONISTS NEAR BATTLE-FORD.[8] The accounts describing the colonists themselves were not flattering either: ONE MORE MISTAKE. ONTARIO WAS NOT REDEEMED FROM THE FOREST BY BARR COLONIES.[9] TRIALS OF THE TRAIL WERE TERRIBLE. WEAK FALL BY THE WAY. WOMEN AND CHILDREN HAD TO ENDURE MUCH MISERY.[10]

Christina could picture the cold, hungry and exhausted little ones plodding along by the burdened wagons; the hardships of the trail. Whether any of the reporters actually got beyond Battleford remains obscure, but they heard the talk and they filed their stories.

In all this Barr had his supporters. Some of the papers reported them. The *Toronto Star* in an editorial said:

He will be blamed for everything that has gone wrong . . . he serves as a buffer between the newcomers and the country, but these people came of their own accord, and if they had not Mr. Barr to vent their feelings on they would, while their periods of homesickness last, condemn the country, the climate, landscape, air and water. . . . He [Barr] will have trouble enough on his hands without encountering an un-friendly Canadian press. . . . At any rate he deserves fair play from Canada and it should not be denied him.[11]

The Reverend John Robbins in London, formerly Barr's advance agent, defended him. And Mr. W. T. R. Preston blamed much of the dissatisfaction on an attempt to hurt the immigration policy of the Laurier government. But this support all came too late.

For Christina, in the home of Jennie Reesor, Isaac's sister, there was small comfort, for Jennie had been brought up by her stepmother Sophia and, like her, considered Isaac and Jack wild and undisciplined. Christina's very presence strengthened this belief. That the colony scheme would be a fiasco was exactly what Jennie expected and she made it plain. Without question she accepted all the charges, the slurs. She always maintained that Isaac made a fortune from the colony scheme, and she never doubted that he was unscrupulous.[12]

As Christina waited for Isaac to return she realized that the sweeping London vision had become an unpleasant Canadian reality. Slowly her awareness grew that though she had not been deceived by Isaac, she had been betrayed by his weakness. She might have left then. She could have supported herself easily in Canada or returned to England, but she waited for Isaac, partly because she still hoped things might come right; partly because she sensed his deep need for her; and partly, perhaps, in spite of the great difference in their ages, because she loved him.

The legend of his dishonesty, that he was a con man, was to come later in the retrospective accounts of colonists, historians and, in particular, Bishop Lloyd. At the time, the newspapers simply stated that he returned the moneys he owed to the colonists. That he had asked the government for a "bonus" or capitation fee for organizing the colony seemed so unremarkable to them that they reported it in a single paragraph, inconspicuously placed.[13]

Isaac and Christina were still in the Toronto area by October fifteenth, though it is likely they had long since left the unsympathetic shelter of Jennie's home.[14] By Christmas they were in Chicago with Willie, Isaac's half-brother.

From Chicago, Isaac wrote yet again to the Deputy Minister of the Interior in Ottawa. In an effort to clear his name he asked for a complete investigation of the Barr Colony affairs. He was still asking for the capitation fee but now he requested that it be used to pay up any just debts that still remained in connection with the colony. As a measure of his own need for money, he foolishly threatened to disclose to the court of inquiry letters "which would make interesting reading in court" that he had from the Canadian immigration officer in Britain, W. T. R. Preston.[15] He must have felt

Grave of Cecil Rhodes near Salisbury, Rhodesia

IN LOVING MEMORY OF
REV. ISAAC MONTGOMERY BARR
LOVED HUSBAND OF
CHRISTINA
DIED JAN. 18. 1937
AGED 89.
ALSO THE ABOVE
CHRISTINA BARR
LOVED MOTHER OF
HARRY & WILLIAM
DIED JULY 2. 1948
AGED 87.

AT REST.

Grave of Isaac Barr in Cohuna, Victoria, Australia

The Barr Colony School, Lloydminster, Saskatchewan

he was threatened if he should return to Canada, for he stated that he would expect the full protection of the American government during his appearance, since he was now an American citizen. The Deputy Minister replied that no investigation was necessary, that he was satisfied with things as they were.[16] As well he might be. All known claims had been paid and a balance of $629.65 remained in the Barr account. The colony was doing very well.

But Barr was not an American citizen, though he had sworn his intention of becoming one in Lapeer County in the State of Michigan in April, 1885, and he obtained a copy of that document again in January, 1906,[17] for what purpose I do not know. I could find no record of his obtaining his final papers.

Undoubtedly Barr needed money. He had given up the role of priest and, at almost fifty-nine, was ill-equipped to earn a living in any other way. During the next two years he turned to what he called "the last refuge of the unfortunate." He became an insurance agent[18] in Dallas post office, Gregory County, South Dakota.[19]

Isaac was fifty-eight and Christina just twenty-four when they were married in Lincoln, Nebraska, by a county court judge.[20] The long delay may have been associated with the complexities, in those years, of freeing himself from his previous marriages. He was no longer a practising clergyman and this latest union was solemnized by a court official. For by now Isaac had cast aside both church and collar.

Part of this rejection was due to his increasing intolerance of "clerical hypocrisy." Even though he had, in a sense, recanted years before, when he apologized to Bishop Hellmuth and said he believed in that long list of dogmas, by now the years had somehow distilled his bitterness against the church. He had long doubted the doctrines, questioned the hierarchy. In addition, the man he now regarded with contempt, Lloyd, had joined the upper echelons of church administration and management.

Gradually it became clear to him what he had always known but refused to recognize: that his defeat had been of his own making; that had he held control for a few short weeks longer the colony's success would have been Barr's success. And the truth became awful and a burden within him. His feeling of personal failure deepened.

Christina, too, regarded Isaac as a failure—a failure to himself and to her—and the thing between them grew, so that eventually they never mentioned the colony. Instead of a proud memory to pass on to their sons it became a sorrow, a humiliation to be hidden from the world.[21]

For two years he managed to earn a meagre living at a job he loathed but by then he could no longer stomach the insurance business, so he moved his wife and infant son to a little farm near the Canadian border at Ferndale, Washington, close to the old parish he had served just before he launched his colony scheme. Barr returned to the same spot from which five years before he had set out to build the empire.

The farmhouse was set close to the seashore in a beautiful and solitary land, where the howling of the coyotes at night seemed only to increase Christina's loneliness. There were few neighbours. At the back door was the ocean and at the front the mountains, half a world away from the London streets and theatres she loved. Money on the small farm was scarce, for Isaac as a farmer was inept and impractical. Christina worked very hard, canning vegetables and fish to feed the family. By then she had a second small son. Often too she had to help Isaac with the outside work, the haying, the animals, the chickens.[22]

As a family they had begun again to build a place in their little community. Isaac became a member of "The Grange," a national farmers' organization, and was appointed delegate to the "Dry Farming Congress" at Spokane.[23] For the moment the Barrs seemed to have settled down, but it was only for the moment.

Early in January, 1910, someone gave Isaac a pamphlet sent out by the government of Victoria, Australia, describing the Murray River Irrigation System just north of Melbourne. The area had been broken up into "irrigation blocks," little seventy-five-acre farms, that would be available for settlement; there was a picture of lush meadows and an attractive bungalow. The prospectus was signed by The Closer Settlement and State Rivers and Water Supplies Commission.

To Isaac, frustrated by his own ineptness and still trying to escape his memories, the words "Closer Settlement" were the siren call of empire. He was off and dreaming. Someone ought to fill this empty part of the British dominion with suitable people, people who would hold the country for the crown. He wrote for more information; he approached the Australian agent in Seattle several times to express his enthusiasm as an intending immigrant.

And he was organizing again too. He founded and became the first president of the American-Australian Settlement and Tourist Club. And, in passing, he assured the agent he had "many desirable and financial friends who were prepared to proceed to Australia on his recommendation."[24]

But this time things were different. Barr had neither the money to start nor the energy to organize another colonization scheme. This time he would go himself and then recommend that the others of his club join him there. And this time he added "Tourist" to its title[25]—just in case.

By early December he had settled his affairs, sold his farm and with Christina and his two children, Harry, five, and William, three, he sailed for Australia, a settler, an immigrant, going to a strange country as part of a colony scheme. After all his sorry experience, here he was starting out to be a colonist himself. Later Barr was to feel that he had been misled; that the conditions he found had not been truly represented to him; that The Closer Settlement Scheme did not live up to the promises it had made.[26]

Had he been a real con man he would have recognized the "pitch."

Sound of a Distant Drum

Actually, my quest for Barr had not begun with a search for the record of his birth. My article on the colony had appeared in December, 1963. All winter long I fretted about the discrepancy in my story. In March I knew I must find the answer by finding the man. I cast my net in many quarters.

Descendants. Who else would know him? Death certificates usually state the next of kin. But where had Isaac died? Some accounts said in the United States and some Australia.

Ivan Crossley had mentioned that a Professor Guy Lyle was writing a book on the colony, had been for years, and that he lived in a certain American city. I, like Isaac, am impressed by titles. Surely a professor would know, especially a professor who was writing a book. So I dispatched a letter to Guy Lyle in care of the university I knew to be in that city. In exchange for his assurance that Barr had died in Australia, I gave him the information that the Mavor Papers existed and where they were to be found.

From a handy atlas I learned the names of Australia's seven states and their capitals and wrote the registrar of vital statistics in each. (He has a different title in each state but Australia has an efficient postal service.) It is impossible to enclose the postage of another country for return mail and the offer to pay any cost connected with the search of records evokes a different response from each state or province. In Australia they search first and ask for payment afterwards.

One by one the states replied. Among their records for the likely years there was no mention of Isaac Barr. And then, about six weeks after all the others, I heard from Victoria. The registrar enclosed a certified copy of Isaac's death certificate and billed me for a trifling fee, a pittance for a priceless record.

Isaac Montgomery Barr, retired clergyman, died January 18, 1937, at McMillans in the Shire of Cohuna, County of Gunbower, of cardiac failure.[1] The location of his grave was named. And his next of kin?

The information on the certificate was explicit. It detailed two marriages: where, at what age and to whom; it listed the full name, order of birth and ages of the issue of each union. The detail was limited only by the amount of the informant's knowledge. Here I first encountered the name Christina Helberg and here I learned what the initial M in Barr's name represented. It was here also that I learned that at the time of his death he had two living sons, Harry Montgomery Baird Barr and William Henry Barr.

Where was McMillans? What was McMillans? An hotel, a post office, a store? I could find it on no map I had, though Cohuna was marked. Knowing the exact date of Barr's death I wrote all the Melbourne newspapers listed in *The Worldmark Encyclopedia of the Nations** asking for the obituary notice. Only *The Age* responded, enclosing a copy from their files. It was in this item that I first found mention of Isaac's intended colonization scheme with Rhodes. I wrote again to the editor asking his advice about where to address the next of kin, at McMillans or Cohuna? His answer: McMillans had been a crossroads post office closed now for many years; I should try Cohuna.

It is not easy to compose a letter to the relatives of a dead man who has been damned by the historians of his country as a thief. How to convince his sons and his widow that, having found them, I was not seeking to exploit their shame and sorrow?

---

*Worldmark Press, Inc. Harper Bros., New York, 1960.

I wrote four letters, one to Mrs. Christina Helberg Barr, one to each son and one to the postmaster at Cohuna telling of the other three and asking that, if they could not be delivered locally, he forward them.

The uncertainty and the waiting were agonizing. By this time I was obsessed with Isaac Barr. I had to know.

Three weeks later came a letter from William Hall Barr (the death certificate had named him incorrectly), Isaac's younger son. It was a touching document, beautifully written, expressing gratitude that someone was at last interested in the story of Isaac Barr, that someone cared about his father's name. He told me that his mother had died some years before, and his brother refused to acknowledge my letter and advised William to do the same, since a revival of the Barr story would only rouse old torments and bring nothing but more shame.

In my elation at having reached Isaac's son I behaved like a stupid boor. I promptly sent off a long letter composed mainly of what I had already found about his father and asking for precise details to fill the gaps. His reply was cool, remote and questioning. Just who was I, anyway, and what were my real motives? Sensationalism? Money? How could he trust me? Frankly, how could he?

Bill's acceptance of me came slowly and, for him, painfully. He wanted very much to believe that someone cared for the truth about his father. I admitted to him that I had written an article about Barr, that I was ashamed of it now and wanted to find out the real story. I did not dare send him a copy and I dreaded the day he might read one. I referred only vaguely to the many accounts and books written about Isaac, without giving him specific titles. He challenged me on the point. He had only *my* word that the accounts were as derogatory as I suggested. So, reluctantly, I listed a few of the books for him, the ones I thought would distress him least. He made the trip — one hundred and seventy miles — to the library in Melbourne just to read them. His hurt that day was brutal.

There followed a lapse of several months in our communication. I busied myself reconstructing the other details of

Isaac's life; Bill tried to recall what he could of his childhood, his family and his father.

I needed Bill by now to make the story whole. I needed him enough that eventually, months later, I sent his wife a copy of *The Promised Land* by C. Wetton,[2] asking her to read it so that she would know the extent of the error that must be set straight. She was to give it to Bill only when she felt he could bear to learn the story it told and only if she thought it would show him why I must write this book. Bill read *The Promised Land* about the same time as he read my article in an old copy of *Maclean's* (thoughtfully sent to him by a relative in Canada). I was no kinder than she; only my motives were different.

In September, 1964, I had suspended work on the Barr book to go with the Canadian Medical Expedition to Easter Island, and to publish in the fall of 1965 *A World Away*,[3] an account of that expedition. This chatty small book proved to be the catalyst that made Bill's acceptance of me possible. I had sent the Barrs a copy that Christmas, 1965, and asked if I might visit them the following March in Australia.

Though we had corresponded for two years, had written about our families and exchanged pictures of our children, it was not only with excitement but real trepidation that I stepped off the train in Cohuna to face Isaac's son. I need not have worried; the entire family, warm, friendly, excited, was there on the platform to greet my husband and me. Later that evening Bill's wife told me quietly, "It was your book that did it. After we read it we knew you." They had decided I could be trusted.

We spent an emotional week with Bill and his wife Phyllis, their daughters Glenys and Janette, and their son Robert. We met Glenys' fiancé and his parents; we listened to Robert's talk of cars and rallys as he went about his work on the small dairy farm; and we were captivated by the gamin charm of Janette, just sixteen. We walked over the paddocks Isaac had farmed, visited the nearby hamlets where he had done business, and talked with oldtimers who remembered him well.

Some of what the family told me went onto tapes; some I recall from a scribbled note, perhaps only a single revealing word caught as we talked. Here, where he had lived for twenty-six years, my picture of Isaac Barr became a collage of colour, of frailties and impatience, of dreams and bitter pride, stuck to that framework of dates and times I had been able to build from old records.

In flat prairie land laced with irrigation canals and trenches, on the seventy-five-acre irrigation block assigned to the Barrs, the meadow grass stood a foot high.

To reach the site Isaac and the family travelled by train north and west from Melbourne, a hundred and seventy miles to Macorna. In a community centred by a village of three hundred there was a general store employing twenty-one, to serve in the foundry, groceries, dry goods, ladies' wear and hardware sections. There they were "dumped" by The Closer Settlement Scheme and from there Isaac had to hire transportation to get to a place where he could buy a horse and wagon. Unlike the Barr colonists, he could get his supplies seven miles away at Cohuna, a crossroads point with a blacksmith's shop and a store, supplied by bullock cart from Macorna.

Nearby farmers raised pigs, cows and fruit enough for themselves and for market. They came to the village for kerosene and supplies but cut their own firewood. It was all so very like the Barr Colony, except that the railway was already there.

The bungalow pictured in the pamphlet was nowhere in sight. On the Barr property stood a two-roomed shack, with walls lined with hessian, the heat supplied by a single small brick fireplace. To Isaac's young wife, who loved pretty things, it was like going back in time. There were no amenities.

When the Murray River Irrigation System began neither authorities nor users knew much about its operation. A Mr. Mead, chairman of The Closer Settlement Board urged, "Use water, all you want!" So the farmers let the water in onto their fields. Within a year the water table rose and all the salt came up through the soil. The fields turned black and died. The young fruit trees withered and the paddocks became a wasteland. In the beginning neither officials nor settlers understood about drainage. As the ruin spread before them the colonists, discouraged and impoverished, abandoned their small farms. Isaac too might have given up but at sixty-five he was too old to start all over again.

When he came to Cohuna he had very little; the farm was financed by the government, and even after he died twenty-six years later it was still hopelessly in debt. Contractors had been putting the irrigation trenches through when the settlers arrived and a charge was made against the land to recover the costs, but Isaac could never pay this off and eventually the government cancelled his debt.

Isaac Barr always worked hard. He was very strong; he could grasp a young tree and pull it up by the roots. But real success eluded him because he was so impractical and so unmechanically minded. He would drop the handle off the separator and Christina or one of the boys would have to come out and put it back on. In spite of this obvious deficiency he fancied himself as an inventor. He designed a metal gadget to hold an axe-head onto the handle. No wedge for him! With his half-brother Willie he had once invented, with conspicuous lack of commercial success, a revolutionary kind of collar stud.

The Barr fortunes did not prosper in Australia. Three years after they arrived Isaac, still plagued by malarial chills, was going blind from cataracts. It fell to Christina and the boys to keep the farm running. "When he plowed he used a single-furrow plow and a sighter peg. He couldn't see well and we'd nip down and move the peg and so he'd plow a crooked furrow. We thought this a great joke but he didn't find it funny."

The two sons walked a mile across the paddocks to the McMillans crossroads school, a one-roomed building with a little house out back. Later there was also a post office and a hall, built by The Closer Settlement, for dancing and social events. These the whole community attended. At a dance or a party the smallest children would be put to sleep in the buggy. Mostly the settlers made their own entertainment. There was a debating society and Isaac would go and win all the debates.

William told me:

Dad had a very loud voice. It used to embarrass us—sort of pulpit tones. He was great at quoting—quoted Shakespeare, especially *Hamlet*:

> ... I could a tale unfold whose lightest word
> Would harrow up thy soul; freeze thy young blood;
> Make thy two eyes, like stars, start from their spheres;
> Thy knotted and combined locks to part,
> And each particular hair to stand on end,
> Like quills upon the fretful porpentine:

And we'd all listen and be all scary like, and shivery. Or Gray's *Elegy*:

> Full many a gem of purest ray serene,
> The dark unfathom'd caves of ocean bear:
> Full many a flower is born to blush unseen,
> And waste its sweetness on the desert air.

He'd do it with tears in his eyes. He was very emotional.

Isaac was also superstitious. He accepted the tale his father told him, that when one of his daughters (Isaac's sister) lay gravely ill William had seen the wraith of his dead wife, Catherine Baird Barr, hovering over the sickbed. And Isaac firmly believed that he had been "warned," though he never specified by whom, before he set sail from England "that there were traitors among the colonists" and that he would have trouble with them. A strange contradiction in a man who preached the scientific way of life and expatiated on the theory of evolution. It was the Celt in him, no doubt.

Church socials too were held in the hall. "Mrs. Sumpter was very fat. She would go to all the church socials. Always carried a big parasol. One day the clergyman moved to open it for her and out tumbled hordes of goodies. But we liked the neighbours in the settlement."

When the boys started school the First World War had begun and they blushed with shame because their mother's maiden name was German, though she had never been to Germany.

And they suffered for their father too. Back of the hall The Closer Settlement had added a small section for a community library. It is strange that at this tiny crossroads in unsettled Australia, in a library that held only a few trifling volumes, should be a book, *Canada As It Is* by John Foster Fraser, written in 1905 and containing just four paragraphs about the Barr Colony of two years before: "I am not going to enter into the savage controversy that arose between the immigrants and Mr. Barr. Sufficient it is to say that they were brought out, according to them, under false pretences, that what little money they had was soon lost, and that lynching is now considered in the North-West a far too agreeable punishment for the Rev. Mr. Barr. I know nothing about Mr. Barr."[4] How the other children taunted them. "Ha! Ha! Your father got kicked out of Canada!" Sometimes in their jeering they called him Ikey. "It used to make me all sort of sad and lonely inside. And sometimes it caused fights too. But it hurts when you are not very old to have something big in your mind to feel badly about." From the gibes of the children there was no defence. "We believed he was a failure too, because mother believed he was a failure. You take your attitudes from your parents."

The boys did well in their studies. Harry was especially good at maths but he left school at thirteen because his help was needed on the farm. As his life moved on he seemed always to resent that he had not had the advantages that others had enjoyed. When he was older he bought the property adjoining his father's. As a member of the shire council he was respected in his community and eventually became the council president. Harry was like his mother in personality and ability; Bill more like his father. "I could read books early. I liked words, but I was less of a businessman than my brother."

Isaac "was a strange man, not very well equipped to deal with the mechanics of living. In some ways he was remote.

He could be a loving and kind father and yet could be cold, stern and forbidding. He could recite poetry with tears in his eyes and yet be unaware of the real needs of his boys." But the generation gap was wide. Isaac would be seventy-five years old when William was still a teenager; more like a grandfather than a father to his sons.

When the Barrs first arrived in Australia and had to buy stock for the farm, Isaac was an easy mark for all the sharp cattle dealers.

They used to watch him coming to the sales and then ply him with a few whiskies. Once he came home with only three cattle for a hundred pounds. He was no businessman, he trusted everyone completely. "I don't think he could spot a crooky when he saw one. To him a man's word was as good as his bond, and he never learned that though he behaved this way others didn't. Over and over again he lost." As the man, impractical, trusting, came into focus I marvelled more and more at the achievement of the Barr Colony. Two thousand people, five thousand miles, in just six months!

Isaac was always in the clouds. Obviously, he should not have been farming. One winter the "Million Club" in Sydney wrote enclosing a pamphlet for settling people. Isaac "spent days on end working out in minutest detail a town plan for the settlement with a circular centre and radiating streets. He could always see the ultimate but achieving it was beyond him."

In later years he became crippled. He was accustomed to milk sitting on a stool with his right leg extended, and one day the cow stepped on it breaking the bones. Now Isaac scorned doctors; said they were a bunch of humbugs, operating when it wasn't necessary. He referred to women who had their tubes cut as "society whores."

The bush nurse came and put a splint on the leg. Then the next day the doctor arrived and applied a cast. A few days later Isaac lifted the bedcovers to show a visitor. "Look what I've done," he said. There beside him lay the cast. He had removed it himself, yet as long as he lived it remained the doctor's fault that the leg was not perfect. In later years, when he was old and weak and needed help, he refused to visit the doctor, so his son would give him a couple of whiskies and lead him to the office. "Yes, he drank, but he was never drunken. He certainly had his troubles. They didn't have tranquillizers in those days."

As his sons knew him, he was almost blind, partially crippled and beset by the onrush of old age; a mere shell of the man he must have been in the full vigour of his manhood.

More and more it was necessary for Christina and the boys to take over the farm and work it to support the family. The adjustment was not easy, for Isaac resented any interference with his ideas and plans. Some violent disagreements resulted, with Harry taking his mother's side and Bill mute and miserable.

The disparity in age between Christina and Isaac did not make things any easier. She wanted to go out to dances and parties, while he was content to stay at home, to have Christina read to him or to have a visit with a neighbour. Chief on his list of favourite friends was Hogan, an Irishman, who used to put away a few. Then he would come to visit Isaac bringing a little pipe with him. They would sit down together in front of the shed and Hogan would tweetle the pipe and dance. They argued endlessly about the Creation in voices that carried as far as the house. Hogan was a Catholic and Isaac would try to convince him about evolution. Hogan always carried a moneybag of sovereigns, which he planted before he died, and no one has ever been able to find them though they dug up the whole place.

Sometimes Isaac played chess with another friend, a Catholic priest. Or Jack Murphy would come. He was from Canada; not a colonist but he had worked in the woods in Northern Saskatchewan and knew the country well. Now, in Australia, he delivered grain. Murphy would arrange to have his rounds finish at the Barr place and then he would say, "Now we'll have a yarn." And he and Isaac would talk about Canada—always about Canada.

"Father had a great knowledge of Canadian history. Sometimes he would preface his remarks with, 'When I was a boy in Canada.' When he did this, we would groan and mutter, 'Here the old man goes again!' But we listened. If ever there was a patriot in the old-fashioned sense of the word it was Isaac Barr."

Politically, he was always a socialist believing in planned communities and co-operative societies. The last of his pamphlets, "The Canadian Co-operative Home Farm Number One"* is a beautifully worked-out plan describing the organization and operation of a self-supporting educational scheme to teach young Englishmen how to farm in Canada, to be self-reliant when cut off from remittances from home. In it he says:

Generally speaking it is recognized today that co-operation or association is the true principle of success in all commercial pursuits . . . . It is believed that members shall find here the training in business, that development of a sense of responsibility and self control, that feeling of mutual dependence, as well as appreciation of the value of money, which shall lead to high success in future life.

Farmers should be public spirited men; they should, in such a democratic country as Canada, where all offices are open to able, conscientious and wide awake men, look forward to a life of public usefulness as well as private gain and enjoyment. Hence it is felt that the management of their own affairs by the members, the discussions and debate in the lecture and entertainment hall, the lectures by public men from time to time, and all the numerous self-directed activities of such a co-operative life, must tend to draw out all that is best in the men and fit them for a life of great usefulness and assured success.[5]

The socialist had dreamed the dream; he had issued the challenge.

Had the story of Isaac's great venture been one of success and triumph his children would have known and remembered much, much more about the details, but as it was one of dismal failure, shattered hopes and cruel disappointment, their youthful minds rejected the whole subject.

---

*See Appendix, page 146.

Neither Isaac nor Christina ever mentioned anyone connected with the colony nor in fact the colony itself, except
for the one reference to Lloyd.

One evening, as we talked, William said:

For many years there was a steamer trunk full of documents
relevant to the colony. I remember now tearing up big
ledger books, to get the few blank pages left. (In those days
we used slates at school, paper was at a premium.) Among
the papers there were long lists giving the names and occupations of the colonists. Looking through them one day I
could not help but think, "No wonder the old man struck
trouble out there." A more unlikely looking list of pioneers
you never saw — clerks, shop assistants, warehousemen,
bookbinders, salesmen, umbrella makers, newsagents, post-
men, small business types.

Termites too had gotten into the trunk where it was
stored. Much of the story of his life was probably there also;
many old letters, photographs, odds and ends, sad reminders
of a life gone by. Sometimes when I used to rummage
through the trunk it filled me with a strange sad feeling. To
me it was a kind of Pandora's box; when opened all the
miseries seemed to flow out.

William asked the questions: Why did Isaac bring all this
stuff to Australia with him, at such expense in freight?
Wouldn't he have destroyed the evidence if he had been
guilty of defrauding the colonists? And he answered them
himself. "I think I know the answer now. It looks to me as
though he had intended to go back some day and clear his
name. But as old age and infirmity crept on him and he had
no money, he resigned himself to his fate. He just didn't
care any more."

After Isaac died William still kept the trunk and its dam-
aged documents. Then one day, shortly after his mother
died, he thought, "What the hell am I keeping these for?
There was no word from Canada when he died. They broke
his heart out there. So I consigned the lot to the flames. He
was my old man and I felt for him."

William still has the flag that flew over the colony,[6] the flag that his father raised at Headquarters Camp that sunrise, May 10, 1903. He saved too the letter from the Governor of the Territories welcoming Barr and his colonists,[7] a few personal documents and the letter from the Archbishop of Canterbury licensing Barr to serve as a priest in England[8] —the certificate Lloyd suggested never existed—along with the commendations from the Bishop of Spokane.[9]

Though the Barrs never really understood why Isaac had spent his small private funds pursuing his dream of colonization they had some conception of why he abdicated:

I can understand why the migrants deposed father as their leader. There must have been so much mismanagement in the carrying out of the expedition they lost their confidence in him and to protect themselves found another man to lead them. . . .

Of course I am not so naive as to imagine that my father was faultless. I can quite understand that in his dream to settle the vast open spaces of the British Empire with British peoples he would think of the honour and glory that would be his. How he would go down in history as the man whose vision it was that helped accomplish this, but surely this would be a perfectly understandable human weakness, a little vanity, not a motive that would be questionable or dishonourable in any way.

Knowing him as I did, I don't think he had any motive in the ordinary meaning of the word. Surely the artist doesn't have to have a motive when he creates his masterpiece, or the visionary when he tries to realize his dream.

As his days declined Isaac continued to dream of settling people in the empty spaces of the empire. He addressed letters to the editors of various newspapers, to government departments and, using a powerful lens to compensate for his near-blindness, laboriously spelled out pamphlets with schemes for the colonization of Australia, dispatching them to various state and dominion personalities.

At his death, just six weeks before his ninetieth birthday, written on the endpaper of the book he had been reading was:

Agrarianism   Wide spaces
               small farms
               city settlements
               not big cities

Local control group
Federal Co-operated Groups
New States
New Organizations
   1. Banks
   2. Co-op stores
   3. Manufacturing
   4. Co-op forestry
   5. Co-op sports
   6. Public Hall
      Schools
      Colleges

Isaac Barr was still building communities.

Even in death his identification with Cecil Rhodes was complete. Isaac, so far as his son knows, left no instructions about his grave but, there in Cohuna, Australia, it is identical in style and structure with that austere slab set high in the Matapos Range in Rhodesia, bearing the one word: RHODES.

The Cup Is Empty Now

Isaac Barr was an insignificant rural clergyman who spent his pastoral days shifting from field to field, always at variance with his superiors. He would have remained insignificant had it not been for his vast scheme of colonizing Canada, the culmination of a lifetime of dreaming "patriotism." The family tradition was right, the childhood experiences were right, even his taste for pomp and display prepared the ground. Rhodes, the Boer War and the coronation of 1902 planted the seeds which reached their fruition in that lonely little scene, the raising of the Canadian flag over "The British Settlement in North Western Canada."

Right from the beginning the seeds of his personal tragedy were there too: impractical, naive, enthusiastic, persuasive, idealistic; a man of action who retreated rather than confront his opposition and fight through to victory.

The Barr Colony itself was a success, but not an easy one. During the first winter food was scarce, or seemed so to people accustomed to a corner greengrocer. Some survived on potatoes, the game they could shoot and the jack rabbits they could snare.[1]

The colonists came ill-prepared for a western winter with freezing temperatures and the occasional blizzard. They lived in sod houses or the wooden shells they were able to set up over hand-dug cellars before the cold set in. Their clothing was unsuitable; patent leather shoes instead of moccasins or felt boots. And they took a lot of chances.

An Englishman doesn't know anything about a blizzard. This one Englishman had built himself a shack, out west of town about eight miles. He was engaged to a very nice girl in the old country and I guess she used to write him a lot of letters. He hadn't been in town for some time and he was anxious to get the mail. . . . Had a short goatskin coat, came down to his hips. Well, he started off to walk. And a blizzard came up. You must remember there weren't houses with lights in them all over the place; there was nothing. Well, this poor devil got completely lost, stayed out all night. In the morning his hands and feet were frozen and he started to crawl. He had crawled quite a distance when he saw some smoke over a little rise. It was from a log house and he started to shout. The homesteader came to the door with a gun in his hand and the lost one shouted to him not to shoot. He looked like a bear with the fur coat and the crawling. The blizzard was over by that time and they hitched up the horses and got him into the town to the hospital tent but all the doctor could do in those days was give him a little morphine. And gangrene set in and the poor devil knew he was dying. I don't know, in those days I think they weren't so good about amputating legs and things. Anyway he asked them to get his mail and they did. "Just put it on my chest here. I can't handle it myself and I don't want anybody to read it to me." And the poor devil died with his mail unopened on his chest.[2]

During the winter of 1903 between twenty to twenty-five-thousand-dollars' worth of stock[3] belonging to the colonists was lost through ignorance of how to care for animals. "We'd built a little stable and we bought some sacks of flour and we put it in the stable to keep dry. This was in the fall and we weren't using the place for the animals yet. There was a slough outside our house and one morning when we woke up we found one of our horses lying on his back with his four feet in the air, real dead. We went to see what was wrong and his nose was all covered with flour. We went to the stable to look at the flour and he had been in there and eaten most of a sack. And then he went and had a drink of water and he blew up. He was just like a balloon."[4]

The Royal North West Mounted Police reported that
winter they looked after "the suffering poor": about seventeen families by direct relief. In the spring of 1904 the
government supplied about five-thousand-dollars' worth of
seed to the colonists to get them started. A year later the
need was met by only one thousand dollars.[5] "It wasn't that
we didn't have any money but we were afraid to spend our
capital. There was nothing coming in and we didn't know
when the railroad would come and when we would have
anything to sell."[6]

Some colonists turned freighter to supply the village
from Saskatoon and they could make about a hundred
dollars a trip. Some collected the old buffalo bones left
from the Indian slaughters and took them by the wagon
load to the railhead to be shipped to Regina to make ferti-
lizer. A few of the single men went off to work in the lumber
camps. But by the spring of 1904 construction of the railroad had begun and there was plenty of work to be had.

By that time, too, some experienced American and Canadian farmers had moved into the district taking up the
railroad lands and the unreserved homesteads. The work
was hard but it was a rich country and for those of the
colonists who stayed there was prosperity. By the end of
1905 bank deposits at Lloydminster totalled a hundred
thousand dollars.[7]

However, many left. When the railroad came through,
land values rose, the world outside was again accessible and,
enriched by the small stake made on the sale of their homesteads, they moved to places like Edmonton to enter
businesses more suitable for them than farming.

The Barr Colony gave tremendous impetus to the settling of the Territories. The quarter of a million dollars the
colonists are said to have left in Saskatoon enriched that
small community of four hundred and fifty inhabitants and
assured its economic development as a centre by providing
a large concentrated market nearby. Business firms in
Edmonton profited by supplying the downstream settlement by barge, and three years later by railroad.

It hastened the financing and construction of the Canadian Northern Railway; these people could not remain cut

off from service, and the community was big enough to make the extension pay. Also, so large a concentration of British people attracted still more to the area,[8] urged on by Barr Colonists enthusiastic about the colony.

St. Mary's,
Southminster,
Lloydminster, Sask., Canada.

January 6, 1906.

MY FELLOW COUNTRYMEN,
Treading on each others' heels in England,

Why not come here where you can reap a rich reward for your labours, become independent, own your own land and enjoy the pleasure of building up a home for yourself under sunny skies? When you come you will not find the everlasting snow we used to associate with Canada, but almost constant sunshine, a fine dry exhilarating air. You will have to work hard in the spring and summer, then comes the joy of the harvest and time for recreation in the winter.

I came out with Mr. Barr's party in 1903. The first winter was considered by Canadians to be an exceptionally hard one, but it was nothing compared to what I was prepared for, the second winter also was simply delightful, just enough snow to make sleighing possible. This was followed by an abundant harvest and now we are into January again and having ideal weather and building operations are going apace.

Although I brought my wife and family with me and owing to existing conditions of things found living very expensive and myself inexperienced, I am very glad I came and only regret I did not come long ago.

Many Canadians and Americans are settling amongst us, and we cannot fail to benefit by their experience and example. . . . I think a lot of valuable space is wasted in some English newspapers as to whether the Englishman is welcome in Canada. I advise the man who thinks he is **not**

welcome to examine himself and he will probably see there
"the rift in the lute."

I have come to stay and am daily answering letters and
enquiries, and inducing by a fair statement of fact many
to come into this part and pointing out that it means work
and this is no place for a lazy man.

Faithfully yours,

Cranburn A. J. Bowen,
Captain Britannia Rifle Association,
Late of Gainford, Darlington, England.[9]

Why, then, were there so many problems?

The colony was much too large. With both Barr and
Lloyd promoting the idea, it grew quite out of hand. "Barr
should have said, 'There will be five hundred. No more.' If
Lloyd went on encouraging more he [Barr] should have said
to Lloyd, 'You look after them!' This was Barr's big
blunder."[10] There was not enough time for planning and
arrangements, especially for one man. The government
refused to hold the reservation beyond the middle of April,
allowing a scant six months from the time the first letters
appeared in the British press until the two thousand were on
shipboard.

And one man did it all: he arranged for the local travel,
for the steamships, for the CPR transportation in Canada;
for the supplies, the farm animals, the implements at the
railhead and at Battleford; for the homestead allotments so
friends could be near friends; for the government agents,
the land guides to be on the site; for the temporary housing
in tents; for groundsheets and blankets; all with no capital
and the indifferent communications of telegraph and slow
mail. Within the time limit set it was an incredible feat.

But Isaac Barr was too naive. He accepted the word of
the president and the third vice-president of the Canadian
Northern Railway, when he met them in their impressive
offices, and he took their *plans* as promises. Not that they

deliberately misled him; he just did not allow for the vagaries of financiers and the uncertainties of surveyors, engineers and construction schedules. He trusted the steam-ship companies, passing on their promises to the colonists. Albeit unconsciously, he depended on Jackson, the ship's packer, he depended on Canadian suppliers, and on his brother Jack Barr in the vast and unorganized territories and he paid dearly for their omissions and errors. It had never occurred to Barr that the change of sailing date imposed by the Canadian government would bring his people to Saint John on the first day of a long-weekend holiday.

The colonists themselves were part of the problem. Their imaginations too had been captured by the imperial dream: the transplantation of a bit of Britain, total and intact, to Western Canada. A settlement *block* sent them too far beyond the railroad and led them to dissipate their means in getting to the site. Many were just too poor to meet the challenge imposed by one hundred and sixty acres of free-grant land. Had the railroad come on schedule this all-British isolation would not have mattered so much. As it was, it made the colonists resistant to the admixture of American and Canadian farmers from whom they could have learned a great deal.

Though there were men of experience among the colonists the majority were totally ignorant of farming methods, let alone western farming methods. "Green, green, green," is the word they use as they recount the colony tales.

And Barr was a poor psychologist. The mantle of "Leader" contributed to his defeat. Had he scrapped his clerical garb and called himself "The Colony Agent" his story might have ended differently. An agent charges fees, an agent is ex-pected to have funds. People expect to pay for the services an agent renders.

He should have known that the prairies are inconceivable to a London haberdasher, that a prairie trail is not a country lane nor a corduroy a bridge. He should have known that clumps of prairie aspen and willow are not trees; that the blackened path of a prairie grass fire is a "bleeding wilderness," that the great empty arch of the prairie sky is not a patch of smoky grey that shows among the chimney-pots. Barr tried to describe what it would be like but their imaginations failed them. Nothing was familiar. Only those who accepted the unexpected, the different, the unknown, remained to be enriched by the abundant land and to enrich it with the talents they brought.

Isaac Barr was a true colonizer and remained one until he died. He saw the crowding and poverty in Britain, characteristic of the time; he knew that large areas of the empire were being settled by people of non-British origin who might lead the country away from that empire. And so clear to him was the message that, despite his own disastrous experience in Canada, he himself became a colonist for this very reason.

The two schemes had much in common. Even the concept was the same: a "settlement block" and "The *Closer* Settlement." Both began with a pamphlet. Both offered property; the one for nothing, the other at a low rate, government financed; both involved a long sea journey and a far venture to a railhead; in both instances some of the colonists felt they had been misled, that conditions had been misrepresented and promises abandoned. Both, but only after years of work, would be rich, productive tracts. Colonizer, colonist, the objective was the same, the idea fixed.

Isaac Barr was tragic in the classic sense. Within his own personality was the weakness that destroyed him: his inability to stand up to a crisis, his need to retreat from a confrontation.

But he was not dishonest. He was neither a con man nor a thief. The stories that are told, and told again, about the Barr Colony are retrospective, based on hearsay, and mainly untrue. It was easy for the colonists in their discomfort to believe the rumours that travelled up and down the trail. Most of the actual newspaper reports are accurate; it is the sensational headlines, devised to capture interest for straight reporting, that are misleading. And the historians have copied the historians who copied some of the colonists and writers about the colony, so that a whole fabric of distortion reads like fact. I have been guilty of this myself, in the original article I wrote. Swayed by McCormick,[11] Pick,[12] and mostly by Wetton,[13] by the Canadian Historical Society accounts,[14] by Tallant,[15] by Hawkes[16] and by Bruce Peel and Eric Knowles,[17] by Grant MacEwan[18] and by Oliver,[19] I too condemned him.

The error is greater and the condemnation all the more reprehensible because all the relevant documents have been available to anyone who cared to search them out.

While Barr destroyed himself, it was Lloyd who really damned him. He rode along on Barr's dream, the chaplain, supporting the colonists' courage, answering their endless questions, patting their heads, free of all blame, free of all responsibility. I do not believe he sought Barr's job; that would have been folly. I am not sure that Lloyd, when he confronted Barr, demanding his resignation as leader, was aware of how close success was, that the transplant was almost completed, that in a few weeks the job would have disappeared and the word leader have become a hollow title.

But by Lloyd's memoir, *The Trail of 1903*, Barr is damned. With calculated malevolence, and infinite care in the words he chose, Lloyd assassinates the man, point by point; he doubts his right to be a priest; he doubts his honesty; he describes his carelessness with other people's money; he tells how the *police* and the *firemen* had to search for Barr all night and how Barr returned to the ship drunken. Using the name I. M. Barr almost as an epithet, he recounts the problems and relates each one to some deficiency on the part of Barr: the iron stoves, the raised prices; I. M. Barr locked in his cabin; I. M. Barr clearing off for the U.S.A.; the government agent who seemed more interested in supporting I. M. Barr than helping the committee to depose him; I. M. Barr who left for parts unknown; the chapter that ends "but—" The memoir goes on, paragraph after scathing paragraph, until the final revelation that the Deputy Minister of the Interior told Lloyd he knew all about I. M. Barr's past, and would have stopped him but it was too late. But Lloyd never states what it was the Deputy Minister knew.

The Trail of 1903, with all its ill-concealed venom, is a sad ending to a distinguished ecclesiastical career. The Bishop of Saskatchewan never could forget that, though he remained with the colony to serve as a missionary, though the town was named for him, the colony remained the Barr Colony and the people still call themselves Barr Colonists. In this sense the colony was Lloyd's tragedy too, and the sadness is oppressive.

Both Barr and Lloyd are dead. For both the cup is empty now. Barr drained its bitter dregs in knowing that his destruction lay within himself; Lloyd in knowing that he could not defeat Barr.

Lloydminster's newest school is named The Barr Colony School, not merely a tribute to the courage and tenacity of the Barr Colonists but an attempt to right an old, old wrong.

Harry Messum, who always believed in Barr, told me:

Barr saw this land settled, with churches and schools. Barr saw this land as a place to escape from the poverty and drudgery of England; a place to build. Nobody else raised a finger to bring it about, only Isaac Montgomery Barr.

And then he is afterwards called a thief. It is a bitter, cruel thing. And I am not the only one among the colonists who feels guilty. Where there are mementos, and rightly so, to Bishop Lloyd, there is nothing to Barr.

An Englishman likes fair play. And the men who got Mr. Barr at Battleford and insisted upon his resignation had no moral right to do so, nor was the prisoner, as you might call Mr. Barr, given a hearing. The school and the mural represent the movement of a people utterly unused to such an action and ashamed that it could have happened in their midst.

As you gather the true facts you cannot have any other thing to say but that Mr. Barr did not get a square deal. The largest group ever to leave the British Isles in one company was established as a success. And the credit and kudos belong to Mr. Barr.

Well, other people have listened and thought about this and felt their shame. That is how the school and that beautiful mural came to be.[20]

For Isaac and Christina, for William and his children also, the cup is empty now.

Appendix

This, Pamphlet Number Three, is an affirmation of Isaac Barr's belief in co-operatives and an example of his ability to plan an organized community in minutest detail.

The Canadian Co-Operative Home Farm Number One
A Practical School of Training in Agriculture and Stock Raising

CANADA FOR THE BRITISH

Prospectus

Now that the British people are at last waking up to the vast importance and splendid possibilities of Canada, especially along the lines of cereal and stock production, not a few are asking this question: What is the best way to gain a preliminary acquaintance with general farming in Canada, before starting for oneself? Experience has shown that it is an important question. Failure too often results from inexperience. There have been other causes for the occasional failure of young men of British birth in Canada, among them a too great reliance in many cases upon remittances from home. If many young Englishmen had been compelled to burn their ships behind them, there would have been fewer failures among them in a country where no one need fail. Travelling throughout the Canadian North-West, one hears of many cases where men started life on farms in that country with nothing but what they earned as they went along, and steadily rising to independence, and not seldom to opulence. There is no reason, of course, why the possession of money should prove a hindrance or a cause of failure, provided that its possessor also has common sense and experience to back it up. How to gain this experience in the shortest time, under the best auspices, with the greatest material advantage, and at the least expense is the question. If, in addition, it could be shown that financial profit could at the same time be compassed there would be found the perfect solution of a problem that has vexed not a few who have given thought to this subject. It is a fact that British youth who have been placed on farms, whether in the United States or Canada, for the purpose of

146

learning farming, often after paying bonuses and a large annual outlay have seldom got their money's worth and too often have left their employers and instructors almost as ignorant of any real knowledge as when they started. What plan shall we try next? The following plan is at least well worth a trial. There may be some drawbacks and difficulties. There always are in such ventures but none that need prove insurmountable. *Solvitur Ambulando.*

THE PLAN

Let, say, 20 young men, earnest of purpose and of good character, unite in a co-operative association. Let them purchase a section of land—640 acres—in a district where they wish finally to settle, and where there is plenty of government land to be homesteaded and railroad land to be bought. It is believed to be better to begin on the unbroken prairie, so that all the conditions of farm life on the prairie may be mastered from the very start.

THE ASSOCIATION A LIMITED LIABILITY COMPANY

The association shall organize themselves into a Limited Liability Co-operative Company under the laws of Canada providing for such similar organizations.

FARM OVERSEER

Let them employ a married farmer of known skill and reputation, to teach them and to direct their operations. This overseer must himself have succeeded as a farmer in the North-West, and his wife must be a competent housekeeper and manager of the dairy department. Such people are to be had in Canada at a moderate salary.

THE FARM HOME

On the co-operative farm the association would erect their co-operative farm home. Comfortable but cheap buildings—house to live in and sheds for stock, to be erected partly of logs and partly of lumber (sawn timber). Much of this work, especially the cutting of the logs and transporting them to the building site, hauling of lumber and the rough building work can be done by the young men themselves, and with the assistance of one carpenter and the farm overseer the cost need not be great.

It is important that the young men should learn to be handy and to help themselves and luxurious quarters should not be sought. Warmth, convenience, and sufficient room are required. Let there be plain furniture—sufficient for comfort, no more. Then stock and implements are needed and can also be co-operatively owned by the association.

ORGANIZATION

(1) The agreement shall be for three years.

(2) There shall be a president, vice-president, secretary, treasurer and bookkeeper all elected by the company from their own number.

(3) All money shall be deposited in a bank in Winnipeg or the nearest town of importance, to the credit of the association and shall be paid out by cheque of treasurer countersigned by the president and vice-president. The association shall be protected by a bond covering deposits, to be taken out by the treasurer in the name of the association, in some Guarantee Society such as exists in England and in Canada, the premium on which shall be paid out of the general fund of the association.

(4) The shares shall be £300 [$1,500] each. This would give a working capital of £6,000. Each man must in addition provide his own passage money and his outfit of clothing besides pocket money for one year.

(5) The organization shall, if possible, be effected in England, but the money shall only be deposited when Winnipeg is reached and the treasurer's bond is written.

(6) No profits shall be divided until the termination of the agreement at the three years covered by the agreement when the co-operative farm shall be sold together with stock, implements, and crops etc. and the proceeds divided.

HOMESTEADS

As soon as the district in which it is proposed to settle is reached, and the site of the farm home chosen the young men should select their free grant (homesteads) of 160 acres each, and enter for the same at the nearest government land office, paying the fee of two pounds, which shall come out of each man's own private funds. In addition to this free grant each man may buy as much more railway or gov't land (if the latter may be bought) adjoining his homestead as his means may permit or aspirations dictate. These free grant farms and purchased farms shall lie around and within easy reach of the central farm, which alone shall be co-operatively owned.

CULTIVATING THE HOMESTEADS

While the members of the association shall be cultivating the home farm, and learning agriculture under the direction of their skilled overseer, a certain proportion of time—say one quarter— shall be given to the fulfilment equally on each homestead of the gov't homesteading conditions, which are very light; but they shall have their residence at the home farm (except as here-inafter provided) and devote three-quarters of their time to the cultivation of the home farm. For this purpose the cultivation of the homesteads, the stock and implements of the association shall be used by the members and it shall be the aim of the members to assist one another in a spirit of true brotherhood. Each man shall be at liberty to hire independent labour for the cultivation of his homestead, and in the event of his doing so may have his own stock and implements on his farm.

INITIAL EXPENDITURE

The initial expenditure would be as follows:

640 acres at £1 per acre	£ 640	0 0
Dwelling house for 20 people built of logs and lumber bungalow style	350	0 0
Sheds for stock, logs, and lumber	250	0 0
Furniture, etc., very plain	200	0 0
6 pairs horses, £60 per pair	360	0 0
6 waggons, £15 per waggon.	90	0 0
6 double harnesses, £6 per pair	36	0 0
6 ploughs, £4 each	24	0 0
2 sets harrows, £5 each	10	0 0
2 brood mares, £25 each	50	0 0
1 double driving harness	8	0 0
1 single driving harness	5	0 0
1 light driving waggon	20	0 0
1 single driving buggy	15	0 0
4 farm sleighs, £5 each	20	0 0
1 driving sleigh	7	0 0
1 hay rake	8	0 0

1 mower	12	0 0
1 self binder	25	0 0
1 land roller	10	0 0
1 cultivator	8	0 0
2 disc harrows, £6 each	12	0 0
Small implements	20	0 0
Carpenter's tools	10	0 0
20 milch cows, £8 each	160	0 0
1 bull	40	0 0
Pigs for breeding purposes	20	0 0
Fowls	5	0 0
Seed for planting 100 acres, first year	20	0 0
Seed for planting 200 acres, second year	40	0 0
Farm Overseer and wife, first year	160	0 0
Ditto, second year	160	0 0
Two female servants, first year, £30 each	60	0 0
Ditto, second year	60	0 0
Provisions for 25 people, first year	500	0 0
Ditto, second year	300	0 0
Oil for lighting, 2 years' supply	30	0 0
Repairs, blacksmith, etc.	30	0 0
Hall for public meetings	60	0 0
Insurance on buildings and stock, £1,000 for 3 years	30	0 0
Premium on £6,000 Bond, three years	100	0 0
Sundries	200	0 0
Total	£4,165	0 0
Capital invested	£6,000	0 0
Initial expenditure	4,165	0 0
Balance on hand	£1,835	0 0

It is desirable to have additional balance on hand for the purchase of additional farm implements such as a steam thresher etc. and also for increase of stock. No charge is here made against capital for salaries, provisions etc. for the third year as it is believed the home farm will prove more than self-supporting at that period; there is indeed a possibility that sufficient sustenance for both man and beast will be raised even the second year. It may be well here to mention that the open prairie supplies sufficient hay and pasture. Certainly with the exception of groceries it should be possible to raise everything needed for domestic consumption, and for farm stock after the first year. This would leave a sufficiently large balance on hand to add to the stock and implements to make improvements in the buildings, and to meet all contingencies. Sheep might be profitably added to the stock, and the raising of horses on a considerable scale might be undertaken. Pigs are very good stock in North-Western Canada, and with plenty of cheap cereals and roots, this brand of farm industry might yield no little profit. Flax is also a profitable crop.

As it is the intention to locate the Co-operative Home Farm in the Proposed British Settlement in the Saskatchewan Valley, where no doubt a creamery would be established in the first year, considerable profit would accrue from the sale of cream. By using a separator the milk, even with the cream extracted, is known to be nutritious food for calves. The homestead being grouped about the central home farm, there would be abundant pasturage and hay for a growing herd of cattle. Thus every branch of farming might be in full swing by the end of the second year, and by the end of the third year the whole home farm of 640 acres might be under cultivation and become a very valuable asset. By the end of this year too each man's homestead would be much improved, all the government conditions of settlement fulfilled, and the patents or deeds secured. It is also hoped and believed that with the completion of the third year the members of the association should be sufficiently initiated into the ways of the country, and be possessed of enough skill in mixed agriculture to be able to manage their own farms, when, with the sale of the home farm, stock, implements, and crops, each should have abundant capital to make a good start in life. They will have taken root, so to speak, in the country, formed part of the community in which they are not strangers and should have the advantage of having as neighbours and friends, their fellow co-operators.

Let us now try to approximately estimate the probable financial standing of the association on the completion of the term of the agreement. The following figures are based upon present prices in the North-West, and in the case of the lands on a prospective valuation, warranted, it is believed, by the present rapid development of the North-West, and the immense expansion of railways. It is proposed to locate the home farm on the proposed line of the Can. Northern Railway.

Approximate Estimate of Results at the End of Three Years Allowing for Possible Increase of Stock etc. Also Wear and Tear on Implements.

640 Acres home farm prospective value £5 per acre	£ 3,200
20 Homesteads improved and patents secured £3 per acre	9,600
Original stock implements and furniture less 25% wear and tear	881
Increase of stock from natural increase and purchase	500
Additional implements	500
Total Value at the end of 3 years	14,681
Capital at the end of three years	14,681
Original Capital	6,000
Increase of Capital	£ 8,681

That is to say that 20 co-operators should at the end of the three years have acquired a knowledge of farming, under the most pleasant auspices and would find themselves with their capital augmented to the extent of £8,681; or to put it another way, each man would have his homestead of 160 acres worth £480 and cash on sale of the home farm etc. £254/1/0: Total £734/1/0.

Thus each man more than doubles his capital in three years, while at the same time acquiring a knowledge of agriculture. No account is here taken of the very probable considerable profit of farming operations the third year, when the whole or greater part of the home farm would be under cultivation; nor is any cognizance taken of the probability that some, if not all, of the members of the association would buy railroad lands adjoining their homesteads, and that this additional land would participate in the general increment of value, and so form an additional profit to be placed to the credit of the project. I am quite willing to submit the above figures to the criticism of any expert.

ORGANIZATION, CONSTITUTION AND GOVERNMENT

At the first meeting of the co-operators, which, if possible shall be held in England, they should organize themselves, adopt their constitution with such by-laws, rules and regulations as may seem necessary.

SELF-GOVERNMENT THE DOMINANT NOTE

The dominant idea of the association will be self-government. It is believed that this will appeal to Britons especially, and that they will respond to self-imposed ideas and ideals. They will thus realize that the life of such an association is not different in its obligations and responsibilities from the life outside, and the welfare of all, and the success of the experiment depend upon each individual; that shirking of work and misconduct must inflict injury upon all, as well as upon the offending member, and also bring reproach upon the British name. It is believed that through self-government, a social conscience shall be awakened that must be of immense value in after life. It is further believed that the results shall be distinctly better, the conduct of all being upon a voluntary basis. This plan will attract men of years of discretion who would not attend an ordinary farm training school, and whose influence would be for good. Strong personalities will result from this self-control, and the young men must acquire a valuable training for both public and private life.

RULES ETC.

There shall be a president, a vice-president, a secretary, treasurer and bookkeeper. None of these officers shall hold office for more than three months at a time (except the president and the bookkeeper, who shall hold office for six months), and may at any time be set aside by a two-thirds vote of the association. Voting shall be by ballot.

There shall be the following committees:

(1) A committee on buying
(2) A committee on selling
(3) A committee on improvements
(4) A committee on constitution and by-laws
(5) A committee on lectures and entertainment
(6) A committee on work
(7) A committee on hired labour
(8) A committee on bill of fare for the table
(9) A committee on new members

These committees shall be elected viva voce by the association in session. The first mentioned member of any committee shall be chairman and shall have power to call the committee together at any time. No committee shall hold office longer than three months.

AMENDMENTS AND CHANGES IN THE CONSTITUTION, RULES ETC.

All changes, alterations, amendments, etc. in the constitution, by-laws, and rules etc., of the association shall be submitted by the appropriate committee to the supreme court, and shall be adopted or rejected by a two-thirds vote.

A SUPREME COURT

All the members of the association shall form a Supreme Court, and shall decide all matters in any way affecting the association or the individual members thereof in their relations to the association. From this decision there shall be no appeal. To this court all committees shall make their reports. No committee shall have power to act independently of the Supreme Court. The regular meetings of the Supreme Court shall be held once a week at a time and place due notice of which shall be given by the secretary. Special meetings may be held on call of the president or any three members of the association.

BOARD OF COMPLAINT AND ARBITRATION

This board shall be composed of the president, vice-president *ex officio,* and one elected member. It shall sit once every week at a time and place to be chosen by themselves, due notice of which shall be given by the secretary. This board shall be a lower court, before which the farm overseer and individual members shall lodge all complaints. It shall have power to call all parties before it to receive evidence, and to adjudicate in all matters. It shall endeavour to arbitrate between members who may have quarrelled, and to bring all offenders to a sense of duty. It may refer any matter to the Supreme Court, to which all members shall have right of appeal from the decisions of the lower court.

WITHDRAWAL OF MEMBERS BY DEATH OR OTHERWISE

Any member may withdraw from the association at any time, but his capital shall remain in the possession of the association. He shall, however, be at liberty to dispose of his stock provided the purchaser be approved by a two-thirds vote of the Supreme Court. No interest shall be paid on the capital of a member who withdraws, the loss of his labour to the association being deemed as more than an equivalent. If any member shall die before the expiration of the three years his capital shall remain in the association, but his heir or heirs may dispose of the same, the purchaser to be approved by the Supreme Court by a two-thirds vote. No interest shall be paid on the capital of any deceased member.

CHARGES AGAINST THE STOCK OF AN EXPELLED OR DECEASED MEMBER, OR ONE WHO SHALL VOLUNTARILY WITHDRAW

The association shall have the right to charge against the stock of an expelled or deceased member, or member who voluntarily withdraws, the sum of 40 pounds per annum for the unexpired term of his membership as compensation for the loss of his labour which it might be necessary to replace. This is felt to be just, inasmuch as the expelled member, or the heir or heirs of a deceased one, would necessarily participate in any increment of value in the property on the dissolution of the association.

EXPULSION OF MEMBERS

No member shall be expelled from the association except by a three-fourths vote of the Supreme Court, and only then after due trial by that court. Persistent violation of the rules of the association and neglect of duty or any serious infraction of the laws of the land, may be followed by expulsion.

REINSTATEMENT OF EXPELLED MEMBERS

Expelled members may be reinstated after application, and on a three-fourths vote of the association.

MARRIED MEN MAY JOIN THE ASSOCIATION

Married men may join the association and shall have the privilege of living on their own homesteads, but they shall be entitled to all the rights of the association, including meals at the farm home.

SINGLE MEMBERS MAY MARRY

The married life being the true life, it is hereby provided that whenever any member of the association desires to marry he shall be at liberty to do so, and may remove from the home farm to his homestead, and enjoy, as he formerly did, all the privileges of membership as herein provided.

DISSOLUTION OF THE ASSOCIATION AT THE END OF THREE YEARS

At the end of three years the association shall dissolve, and the property, both real and chattel, shall be sold for the benefit of the association. The Supreme Court shall, by a two-thirds vote, decide upon the price to be placed upon the home farm, which may be sold as a whole or in part, and for cash, or on such terms as the Supreme Court shall decide by a two-thirds vote. The chattel property shall likewise be disposed of in the same manner. It is especially provided, however, that individual members of the association shall have the first right to buy land or chattels on the terms fixed by the Supreme Court.

THE FARM OVERSEER

It shall be the duty of the farm overseer to arrange a program of work for each week and to submit the same to the chairman of the appropriate committee. He shall also oversee all work on the home farm and homesteads, giving such advice and rendering such assistance as he may find time and opportunity to give. It shall also be his duty to advise with the various committees and assist them in their departments. He shall further deliberate with the Supreme Court and sit with the various committees when requested to do so by the president and the various chairmen. He shall not have any vote. The overseer shall be furnished with a pony and saddle, or road cart, to enable him to quickly reach all points where work is in progress.

THE FARM OVERSEER'S WIFE

It shall be the duty of the overseer's wife to furnish a weekly bill of fare to the table committee for approval, and also to supply the purchasing committee each week with the list of goods to be purchased. It shall also be her duty to properly care for all food supplies and to oversee all household arrangements, making of beds, mending of apparel, and so forth. The domestic help shall be subordinate to her, but she shall only hire or dismiss such help with the approval of the committee on hired help.

HOUSES FOR MARRIED MEN

Married men who enter the association shall erect their houses on their homesteads at their own expense, but inasmuch as they shall be bound under the terms of the agreement to contribute their fair share to building on the home farm, they must pay in to the general fund a sum of money which would represent the time employed in building their own houses, at the rate of wages generally paid in the country for farm labour. This should be decided by a two-thirds vote of the members.

MEALS FOR MARRIED MEN

As married men may desire to take at least two meals at home each day, they should be entitled to be paid a sum annually out of the general fund, which shall be a fair equivalent, the sum to be decided by a two-thirds vote of the members.

PARENTS OR GUARDIANS MAY HOLD STOCK IN THE ASSOCIATION

Some parents or guardians may desire to hold stock in their own names for the benefit of sons or wards. It shall be expressly provided that they may do so. The arrangement, however, cannot apply to the homesteads, which can only be entered for in the names of the members of the association.

AGREEMENT BETWEEN THE FARM OVERSEER AND THE MEMBERS OF THE ASSOCIATION

There should be a written agreement between the members of the association and the overseer, which shall specify the duties to be performed by the overseer, and which shall also provide that six months' notice shall be given on either side in order to terminate the agreement.

PROVISION FOR THE EXTENSION OF THE LIFE OF THE ASSOCIATION

Provision shall be made in the articles of incorporation for extending the life of the association beyond the term of three years, provided the majority of the members may decide to carry on the co-operative home farm. This, however, could only be done by buying out and paying cash in full to the retiring members of the association for their shares.

A LIBRARY

It is hoped that individual members and their friends, as well as public bodies and friends of such an experiment, may donate or lend books for the use of the association, with the understanding that the library shall also be placed at the disposal of the community, in which the co-operative home farm shall be located, and so be a means of spreading knowledge and light, especially on proper methods of farming and stock raising, generally, among the people.

A POSSIBLE AGRICULTURAL COLLEGE
AND EXPERIMENTAL FARM

It is realized that, as the country develops and population increases, the home farm might, on the dissolution of the association, be converted into a permanent institution of value to the community, and that it might be taken over by the local government to be conducted as an agricultural college. Its value from the start, even under its co-operative management, to the community as a whole, would no doubt be very great. It might, and it is hoped would, become a centre of enlightment and progress.

A LECTURE AND ENTERTAINMENT HALL

It is provided in these articles of agreement that there shall be a lecture and entertainment hall on the home farm, where public lectures may be given from time to time, by public men, especially on subjects connected with scientific farming, stock raising, creameries, etc. It shall be the duty of the committee on lectures and entertainment to make this provision, also to arrange for debates, readings, recitations, and musical evenings, and whatever else may add to the profitable and innocent enjoyment of the members of the association. It will also be the object of the association to make this hall of entertainment a centre of enlightenment for the whole community, so that the home farm shall be found to be a blessing to all the people grouped about it. Thus, a demand will be gradually created in the minds of the people for a permanent agricultural training school which, if accomplished, will mean also a larger value in the property cn the dissolution of the association. It is further provided that this hall may, on a two-thirds vote of the members, be used for religious purposes.

DISPOSITION OF THE PRODUCTS OF THE HOMESTEADS, ETC.

It is to be noted that each homestead is to be cultivated only to the extent required under the Canadian Homestead Act, and it is hereby provided that the products of these homesteads shall be kept separate from the products of the co-operative home farm; that the proceeds of their sale shall not go into the general fund, but shall form a private fund for each man's private use. In addition each member of the association shall be entitled to draw after the first year, from the general fund, at the rate of one pound per month, and shall be furnished, after the first year, with necessary clothing from the common fund, all to draw alike for this purpose. The association may purchase, at market prices, the products of their homesteads.

HOLIDAYS

All the members shall be entitled to a rest from unnecessary labour on Sundays and public holidays, and also on any other days the Supreme Court shall by a majority devote to rest and recreation.

RELIGION AND ITS OBSERVANCES

It shall be the aim of the association to pay that reverence to religion and the proper observance of the same which shall make for order and sobriety in the community.

LAW AND ORDER

As lovers of law and order and all that makes for the same, this association is pledged to a due respect for the laws of the land, and will do what in them lies to uphold the same both among themselves and others.

ADVANTAGES OF SUCH A CO-OPERATIVE FARM AND FARM HOME

Generally speaking, it is recognized today that co-operation or association is the true principle of success in all commercial pursuits. It has been found more difficult to apply it to farming but where tried in this connection it has worked good results. In this special case it is hoped that it would prove a success. It is believed that the members, through co-operation and self-government, shall find here the training in business, that development of a sense of responsibility and self-control that feeling of mutual dependence, as well as appreciation of the value of money, which shall lead to high success in future life.

Farmers should be public-spirited men; they should, in such a democratic country as Canada, where all offices are open to able, conscientious, and wide awake men, look forward to a life of public usefulness as well as private gain and enjoyment. Hence it is felt that the management of their own affairs by the members, the discussions and debates in the lecture and entertainment hall, the lectures by public men from time to time, and all the numerous self-directed activities of such a co-operative life, must tend to draw out all that is best in the men, and fit them for a life of great usefulness and assured success.

(REV.) I. M. BARR

Late curate-in-charge
St. Saviour's Church
Tollington Park,
London, N.

Notes

THE BEGINNING

1. Mavor Papers, University of Toronto Rare Books Collection.
2. F. Ivan Crossley, Barr Colonist, recorded interview.
3. Birth certificate Harry Montgomery Baird Barr. State of Nebraska, 1907.
4. Rev. Frank Peake, *Isaac Barr: Missionary Extraordinary,* Canadian Church Historical Society (London: Vol. VI. No. 1, March, 1964).

A SENSE OF HISTORY

1. Synod Records, Presbyterian Church in Conjunction with the Church of Scotland. Appendix to Synod Meeting, Sept. 15, 1847.
2. Archie King, Hornby, Ontario. Personal communication.
3. William Hall Barr, son of Isaac Barr.
4. Registry of Deeds, Halton County, Milton, Ontario.
5. Acts and Proceedings of the Twelfth General Assembly of the Presbyterian Church in Canada. Hamilton, June, 1886.
6. Document in possession of Mrs. Helen Thompson, niece of Isaac Barr.
7. *See* ref. 1.
8. William Hall Barr.
9. Helen Thompson. Personal communication.
10. Rev. Thomas Radcliff (ed.), *Authentic Letters from Upper Canada* (Toronto: The Macmillan Co. of Canada, 1953).
11. *See* ref. 5.
12. Rev. Ross Cameron, former Moderator, Presbyterian Church of Canada. Personal communication.
13. Archie King, Hornby.
14. Helen Thompson.
15. William Hall Barr.
16. Helen Thompson.
17. E. C. Kyte (ed.), *Old Toronto,* (Toronto: The Macmillan Co. of Canada, 1954), p. 298.
18. William Hall Barr.
19. *See ref.* 17.
20. William Hall Barr.
21. Helen Thompson.
22. William Hall Barr.
23. Mrs. Phyllis Smythe, grandniece of Isaac Barr.
24. William Hall Barr.
25. Helen Thompson.

26. *Ibid.*
27. Gavin Hamilton, *The Log School* (Goderich: Signal-Star Press, 1939).
28. Helen Thompson.
29. William Hall Barr.

THE TROUBLE WITH BISHOPS

1. William Hall Barr.
2. *Ibid.*
3. J. Grant Morden, Principal, Huron College. Personal communication.
4. James J. Talman, *Huron College, 1863-1963* (London: Huron College, 1963).
5. *Ibid.*
6. *Ibid.*
7. A. H. Crowfoot, *This Dreamer: Life of Isaac Hellmuth, Second Bishop of Huron* (Vancouver: Copp Clark, 1963).
8. George Jacob Low, *A Parson's Ponderings,* cited by James J. Talman, *Huron College.*
9. Church Register, All Saints' Church, Windsor, Ontario.
10. *See* ref. 4.
11. *See* ref. 9.
12. Helen Thompson.
13. Letter from Isaac M. Barr to his aunt.
14. City Directory, City of Toronto, 1870.
15. Helen Thompson.
16. The Registrar, University of Toronto.
17. Vestry Record, Trivett Memorial Church, Exeter, Ontario.
18. *Ibid.*
19. William Hall Barr.
20. *See* ref. 17.
21. Diocesan Records, Diocese of Huron, London, Ontario.
22. *Ibid.*
23. William Hall Barr.
24. Vestry Record, Point Edward and Wilderness, Brights Grove, Ontario.
25. Helen Thompson.
26. William Hall Barr.
27. *See* ref. 21.
28. *Ibid.*
29. William Hall Barr.
30. *See* ref. 21.
31. *Ibid.*
32. William Hall Barr.
33. State of Michigan, County of Lapeer, Circuit Court.

THE AMERICAN YEARS

1. Diocesan Records, Diocese of Michigan, Detroit.
2. William Hall Barr.
3. The Hon. Mr. Justice J. L. McLennan, Supreme Court of Ontario. Personal communication.
4. Archives, Department of National Defence, Ottawa: War record of Harry Baird Barr.
5. Diocesan Records. Diocese of Tennessee, Memphis.
6. *Ibid.*
7. *Ibid.*
8. William Hall Barr.
9. *Ibid.*
10. *See* ref. 5.
11. *See* ref. 4.
12. Records of the Auditor, Whatcom County, Bellingham, State of Washington.
13. Doreen Johnson, grandniece of Isaac Barr.
14. Harry Messum, Barr Colonist.
15. J. G. Lockhart and C. M. Woodhouse, *Cecil Rhodes, The Colossus of Southern Africa,* (New York: The Macmillan Co., 1963).
16. *Ibid.*
17. *Ibid.*
18. Documents in possession of William Hall Barr.
19. E. E. Burke, Director National Archives, Southern Rhodesia, Salisbury, Rhodesia. Personal communication.
20. The Curator, Rhodes Library, Oxford, England.
21. "A Queenly Memorial," *Daily Reveille,* New Whatcom, Washington, February 5, 1901.
22. *See* ref. 18.
23. Archives, University of Saskatchewan Library, Saskatoon.

PANOPLY OF EMPIRE

1. *Fortnightly Review,* Volume for 1902: Lord Salisbury, Speech to the Primrose Club, London, England.
2. Conference of Colonial Prime Ministers, Hotel Cecil, London, England. Cited in editorial, *Toronto News,* August 13, 1902.
3. "Sigma," *Fortnightly Review,* 1902.
4. *Ibid.*
5. Mary Arnold-Forster, *A Memoir of H. O. Arnold-Forster* (London: Edward Arnold, 1910).
6. Harry Messum.
7. Public Archives, Ottawa.

8. George Exton Lloyd, letter to *The Times*, London. Public Archives.
9. George Exton Lloyd, *The Trail of 1903, The Lloydminster Times*, 1940.
10. Pamphlet No. 1. Archives, University of Saskatchewan, Saskatoon.
11. *Saskatchewan Herald*, November 5, 1902.
12. Pamphlet No. 2. Archives, University of Saskatchewan, Saskatoon.
13. Harry Messum.
14. *See* ref. 9.
15. J. A. Smart, Deputy Minister of the Interior, to Lord Tennyson's Committee, enquiring into "Agricultural Settlements in the British Colonies."
16. Archives, University of Saskatchewan, Saskatoon.
17. *Ibid.*
18. Mrs. W. S. Topott, Barr Colonist.
19. *See* ref. 16.
20. *Ibid.*
21. *See* ref. 9.
22. *See* ref. 16.
23. Letter signed by J. A. Smart, Deputy Minister of the Interior, dated August 25, 1903. Public Archives.
24. *See* ref. 16.
25. *Ibid.*

A PAIR OF PRIESTS

1. Lloyd's *Registry of Shipping*, London.
2. Archives, University of Saskatchewan, Saskatoon.
3. F. Ivan Crossley.
4. Harry Messum.
5. *Ibid.*
6. *Toronto Globe*, April 13, 1903.
7. F. Ivan Crossley.
8. *Ibid.*
9. George Exton Lloyd, *The Trail of 1903*.
10. Harry Messum.
11. *Ibid.*
12. Dr. Frank H. Thorne, Barr Colonist.
13. *Toronto News*, April 14, 1903.
14. Harry Messum.
15. *See* ref. 9.
16. Harry Messum.
17. Archives, University of Saskatchewan. Letter dated March 10, I. M. Barr to colonists.

18. *See* ref. 9.
19. Archives of the Canadian Pacific Railways.
20. *See* ref. 9.
21. *Ibid.*
22. *Toronto News,* April 13, 1903.
23. *See* ref. 9.
24. Harry Messum.
25. Dr. Frank H. Thorne.
26. F. Ivan Crossley.
27. *See* ref. 9.
28. Dr. Frank H. Thorne.
29. *See* ref. 9.
30. Dr. Frank H. Thorne.
31. F. Ivan Crossley.
32. *Ibid.*
33. *See* ref. 13.
34. Passenger list, SS *Lake Manitoba.*
35. *See* ref. 13.
36. *Toronto News,* April 6, 1903.
37. *Saskatchewan Herald,* April 8, 1903.
38. *Toronto Star,* April 22, 1903.
39. *Saskatchewan Herald,* March 4, 1903.
40. Lord Tennyson's Committee.
41. Harry Messum.
42. Letter dated Battleford, June 8, 1903, signed W. S. Bromhead. Archives, University of Saskatchewan.
43. *Manitoba Free Press,* April 22, 1903.
44. Document in possession of William Hall Barr.
45. *Manitoba Free Press,* April 22, 1903.
46. *See* ref. 38.
47. F. Ivan Crossley.
48. Lachlan Taylor.
49. *Ibid.*
50. Harry Pick, *Next Year* (Toronto: The Ryerson Press, 1928).
51. Pamphlet No. 2. Archives, University of Saskatchewan.
52. *Toronto Star,* April 21, 1903.
53. *Toronto Star,* April 24, 1903.
54. Bruce Peel and Eric Knowles, *The Saskatoon Story* (Saskatoon: Melville A. East, 1952).
55. *Toronto Globe,* May 4, 1903.
56. *See* ref. 9.

THE BARR COLONY

1. Letter from Capt. A. M. Black to Miss C. Morley, Nottingham. Archives, University of Saskatchewan.
2. F. Ivan Crossley.
3. *Ibid.*
4. Harry Pick, *Next Year.*
5. Surveyors' Map. Public Archives.
6. Pamphlet No. 2. Archives, University of Saskatchewan.
7. Public Archives.
8. Lachlan Taylor.
9. F. Ivan Crossley.
10. *See* ref. 7.
11. *Ibid.*
12. Archives, University of Saskatchewan.
13. George Exton Lloyd, *The Trail of 1903.*
14. J. H. McCormick, *Lloydminster or 5,000 Miles with the Barr Colonists,* (London: Drane's [Ye Olde Ste. Bride's Presse], 1924).
15. *See* ref. 13.
16. Letter from Dr. Amos to Bishop Lloyd cited in *The Trail of 1903.*
17. Helen Thompson.
18. Flag in possession of William Hall Barr.
19. Questionnaire, Archives, University of Saskatchewan.
20. Comparison of advertisements, *Saskatchewan Herald,* February and April, 1903.
21. *See* ref. 6.
22. G. R. Stevens, *History of The Canadian National Railways,* Vol. II. (Toronto: Clarke Irwin, 1960-62).
23. *Saskatchewan Herald,* March 18, 1903.
24. Pamphlet No. 4. Document in possession of Mr. Thomas Parr, Lloydminster.
25. *Ibid.*

THE ABDICATION

1. F. Ivan Crossley.
2. Mrs. W. S. Topott.
3. Lachlan Taylor.
4. George Exton Lloyd, *The Trail of 1903.*
5. The Dominion Meteorological Service. Personal communication.
6. *Saskatchewan Herald,* May 20, 1903.
7. *See* ref. 4.
8. *Toronto Globe,* May 19, 1903.
9. *See* ref. 4.

10. Lord Tennyson's Committee.
11. Dr. Frank H. Thorne.
12. Letter dated June 2, 1903, from George Exton Lloyd to J. A. Smart, Deputy Minister of the Interior. Public Archives.
13. *See* ref. 4.
14. Dr. Frank H. Thorne.
15. Letter dated July 21, 1903, from George Exton Lloyd to all colonists, Lloydminster. Public Archives.
16. Archives, University of Saskatchewan.
17. *See* ref. 4.
18. Public Archives, R. F. Chisholm.
19. *Saskatchewan Herald*, June 3, 1903.
20. Public Archives.
21. Dr. Frank H. Thorne.
22. *See* ref. 20.
23. *See* ref. 10.
24. *See* ref. 20.
25. *See* ref. 10.
26. *Ibid.*
27. *Saskatchewan Herald*, April 22, 1903.
28. *See* ref. 10.
29. *Saskatchewan Herald*, February 25, 1903.
30. *Saskatchewan Herald*, April 1, 1903.
31. *See* ref. 10.
32. *Ibid.*
33. Bruce Peel and Eric Knowles, *The Saskatoon Story.*
34. *See* ref. 4.
35. Dr. Frank H. Thorne.
36. F. Ivan Crossley.
37. Dr. Frank H. Thorne.
38. *See* ref. 16.
39. Dr. Frank H. Thorne.
40. *Manitoba Free Press*, July 8, 1903.
41. Letter from Peter Paynton, December 10, 1905, to Professor Mavor.
42. Harry Pick, *Next Year.*
43. John Hawkes, *The Story of Saskatchewan and Its People* (Regina: S. J. Clark Publishing Co., 1924), pp. 765-76; 71-72.
44. Dr. Frank H. Thorne.
45. F. Ivan Crossley.
46. The Mavor Papers.
47. *See* ref. 4.
48. Original documents in possession of William Hall Barr.
49. *See* ref. 4.
50. *Ibid*

51. *Ibid.*
52. William Hall Barr.
53. *See* ref. 4.
54. *See* ref. 18.
55. *Manitoba Free Press,* July 7, 1903.
56. *Toronto Star,* July 15, 1903.
57. Public Archives.
58. Pamphlet No. 2. Archives, University of Saskatchewan.
59. *See* ref. 40.
60. William Hall Barr.
61. Helen Thompson.
62. William Hall Barr.

THE BITTER YEARS

1. Dr. Frank H. Thorne.
2. Birth Certificate of Christina Helberg, Somerset House, London.
3. William Hall Barr.
4. Passenger list, SS *Lake Manitoba.*
5. William Hall Barr.
6. Helen Thompson.
7. *Toronto News,* June 8, 1903.
8. *Toronto Globe,* May 19, 1903.
9. *Toronto Telegram,* April 30, 1903.
10. *Toronto News,* May 6, 1903.
11. *Toronto Star,* April 20, 1903.
12. Helen Thompson.
13. *Toronto Telegram,* July 15, 1903.
14. Letter to W. D. Scott from I. M. Barr. Public Archives.
15. Letter to Hon. Jas. A. Smart. Public Archives.
16. Letter Hon. Jas. A. Smart to Rev. I. M. Barr, Chicago, Ill., January 4, 1904. Public Archives.
17. Document in possession of William Hall Barr.
18. William Hall Barr.
19. Document in author's possession.
20. *Ibid.*
21. William Hall Barr.
22. *Ibid.*
23. Letter from Mayor of Town of Ferndale, Washington, October 1, 1910. In possession of William Hall Barr.
24. Letter to Hon. Sir W. J. Line, K.C.M.B., M.P., Melbourne, Australia. In possession of William Hall Barr.
25. Letter from Mayor of Town of Ferndale, Washington, October 31, 1910. In possession of William Hall Barr.
26. William Hall Barr.

168   NOTES FOR PAGES 123 TO 145

SOUND OF A DISTANT DRUM

1. Document in author's possession.
2. C. Wetton, *The Promised Land* (*Lloydminister Times*, 1955).
3. Helen Evans Reid, *A World Away: A Canadian Adventure on Easter Island*. (Toronto: The Ryerson Press, 1965).
4. John Foster Fraser, *Canada As It Is* (London: Cassell & Co., 1905).
5. "Canadian Co-operative Farm Home Number One." Pamphlet No. 4. Archives, University of Saskatchewan.
6. Flag identified as authentic by Public Archives. Personal communication in possession of author.
7. Letter dated April 18, 1903, from Governor Forget, Government House, Regina, to Rev. I. M. Barr.
8. Document dated February 4, 1902, in possession of William Hall Barr.
9. Letter dated December 12, 1901, from Bishop of Spokane to Archbishop of Canterbury. In possession of William Hall Barr.

Unless otherwise stated the material in this chapter is from letters from and interviews with William Barr.

THE CUP IS EMPTY NOW

1. Mrs. W. S. Topott.
2. F. Ivan Crossley.
3. Lord Tennyson's Committee.
4. F. Ivan Crossley.
5. Letter dated December 16, 1905, from J. Allen Smith, Commissioner of Immigration, to Professor Mavor.
6. Dr. Frank H. Thorne.
7. C. W. Spears, November 18, 1905, to Professor Mavor: Mavor Papers.
8. C. R. Stevens, *The Canadian National Railways*, Vol. II.
9. The Mavor Papers.
10. Harry Messum.
11. J. H. McCormick, *Lloydminster*.
12. Harry Pick, *Next Year*.
13. C. Wetton, *The Promised Land*.
14. "The Coming of the Barr Colonists." Annual Report, Canadian Historical Association, 1926.
15. C. Tallant, "The Break with Barr. An Episode in the History of the Barr Colony" (*Saskatchewan History* 6:41-6, Spring, 1953).
16. John Hawkes, *The Story of Saskatchewan and Its People*.
17. Bruce Peel and Eric Knowles, *The Saskatoon Story*.
18. Grant MacEwan, *Between the Red and the Rockies* (Toronto: University of Toronto Press, 1952).
19. C. B. Oliver, *Canada and Its Provinces*, Volume XIX, Adam Shortt (ed.). (Edinburgh: printed for the Publishers' Association of Canada, Ltd., 1914-17).
20. *See* ref. 10.

Bibliography

ARNOLD-FORSTER, Mary. *A Memoir of H. O. Arnold-Forster*. London: Edward Arnold, 1910.

Barr Colony Diamond Jubilee, The. The Meridien Booster, Lloydminster, 1963.

BERTON, Pierre (ed.). *Historic Headlines.* Toronto: McClelland and Stewart, 1967.

BURROWS, C. L. *Hands Across the Sea.* Bournemouth, England; Brights Ltd., 1912 [?].

COPPING, A. E. *The Golden Land.* London: Hodder & Stoughton, 1911.

CORBETT, E. A. Unpublished manuscript of a book on the History of Alberta and Saskatchewan, 1964. In the possession of Mr. Alec Messum.

CROSSLEY, F. Ivan. *My Life and Experiences with The Barr Colony.* Winnipeg: *The Western Producer,* 1968.

CROWFOOT, A. H. *This Dreamer: Life of Isaac Hellmuth, Second Bishop of Huron.* Vancouver: Copp Clark Publishing Co., 1963.

FRASER, John Foster. *Canada As It Is.* London: Cassell, 1905.

GREEN, Gavin Hamilton. *The Log School.* Goderich: Signal-Star Press, 1939.

HAWKES, John. *The Story of Saskatchewan and Its People.* Regina: S. J. Clark Publishing Co., 1924.

HIEMSTRA, Mary. *Gully Farm.* Toronto: McClelland and Stewart, 1955.

KYTE, E. C. (ed.). *Old Toronto.* Toronto: The Macmillan Co. of Canada, 1954.

LLOYD, George Exton. *The Trail of 1903.* Lloydminster: *The Lloydminster Times,* 1940.

LOCKHART, J. G. and WOODHOUSE, C. M. *Cecil Rhodes, The Colossus of Southern Africa.* London: Macmillan, 1963.

MCCORMICK, J. Hanna. *Lloydminster or 5000 Miles with the Barr Colonists.* London: Drane's (Ye Olde Ste. Bride's Presse), 1924.

MCCOURT, Edward. *Saskatchewan.* Toronto: The Macmillan Co. of Canada, 1968.

MACEWAN, Grant. *Between The Red and The Rockies.* Toronto: University of Toronto Press, 1952.

MAVOR, Professor James. *My Windows on the Street of the World.* London: Dent, 1923.

Narratives of Saskatoon by Men of the City, 1882-1912. Saskatoon: University of Saskatchewan Bookstore, 1927.

OLIVER, C. B. *Canada and Its Provinces;* Vol. XIX, Adam Shortt (ed.). Edinburgh: printed for the Publishers' Association of Canada, Ltd., 1914-17.

PEAKE, Rev. Frank. *Isaac Barr: Missionary Extraordinary.* Canadian Church Historical Society, Vol. VI, No. 1. London: March 1964.

169

PEEL, Bruce and KNOWLES, Eric. *The Saskatoon Story.* Saskatoon: Melville A. East, 1952.

PICK, Harry. *Next Year.* Toronto: The Ryerson Press, 1928.

RADCLIFF, Rev. Thomas (ed.). *Authentic Letters from Upper Canada.* Toronto. The Macmillan Co. of Canada, 1953.

Rendall Letters, The. Canadian Historical Association, Annual Report, 1926.

STEVENS, George Robert. *The Canadian National Railways,* Vol. II. Toronto: Clarke Irwin, 1960-62.

TALLANT, C. "The Break with Barr." *Saskatchewan History*—6:41-6. Spring 1953.

TALMAN, James J. *Huron College 1863-1963.* London: Huron College, 1963.

WETTON, C. *The Promised Land.* Lloydminster: *Lloydminster Times,* 1955.

Files from the following newspapers:

Edmonton Bulletin
The Lloydminster Times
The Manitoba Free Press
Montreal Gazette
Ottawa Citizen
The Saskatchewan Herald
The Saskatoon Star-Phenix.
The Toronto Daily Star
The Toronto Globe
The Toronto News
The Toronto Telegram

Index

ADAMS, Gilbert, 11
Age, The, Melbourne, 124
Alberta, 1
All Saints' Church, Windsor, Ont.,
    22
American-Australian Settlement
    and Tourist Club, 121
Anglican Church, 20
Archbishop of Canterbury, 41, 108,
    109, 134
Archives—
    Public, of Canada, 112
    University of Saskatchewan, 94
Atonement, The, 31
Auld Kirk, 8
Aurora, 14
Australia, arrival in, 130; Closer
    Settlement and State Rivers and
    Water Supplies Commission,
    The, 121, 126-127, 142; Cohuna,
    Victoria, 123, 126-127, 135;
    Debating Society, 128;
    Government of Victoria, 123;
    pamphlet, 120; Melbourne, 121,
    124; Murray River Irrigation
    System, 121, 126

BAGGAGE, 66, 76
Baird, Captain John, 19, 37
Bank drafts, 79
Bank of Montreal, 101
Barr, Barr Black Sheep, 82
Barr, Catharine Baird, 10, 12, 13,
    14, 15, 128
Barr, Christina Helberg, 52, 87-89,
    114-118, 120-121, 123-124, 127,
    131
Barr church 10, 16, 17
Barr Colony School, 144
Barr Conference Fiasco, 97
Barr, Dora Kathleen, 24, 26
Barr, Eliza Taylor Weaver, 6, 23,
    33, 35
Barr, Emma L. Williams, 35
Barr Farm (Hornby, Ont.), 10
Barr, Gertrude, 29, 36
Barr, Glenys, 125
Barr, Harry Baird, 26, 35
Barr, Harry Montgomery Baird, 6,
    120-121, 123, 129, 131
Barr, Isaac Montgomery,
    abdication, 92, 97-99, 105-106,
    134; American citizenship, 31,

33; application to become
    American citizen, 31, 33; Barr
    Colony scheme, 1; birth, 7, 10;
    capitation grant, Dominion
    government, 110, 112;
    colonization scheme with
    Rhodes, 39, 40-41; commissions,
    79, 102-103; con man, 3, 118,
    121, 142; co-operatives, 116,
    132, 135; death, 123; deposed,
    95-96, 117, 134; doctors, opinion
    of, 32, 130, 131; doctrines
    questioned; Atonement, 31,
    Fall of Man, 27, 31, Trinity, 31;
    documents and papers, 133;
    drinking, 67, 107, 131;
    education, 14-15, 20-23, 26;
    encamped at Battleford, 99,
    112; gives up all homestead
    rights, 97; health: blindness,
    131, crippled, 130, malaria, 34;
    inheritance, 19; "Leader, The,"
    46, 62, 65, 77, 90, 96, 141;
    leaves colony (Lloydminster),
    94; licence from Archbishop of
    Canterbury, 109; life
    threatened, 88; marriages:
    (1) Eliza Weaver, 23; (2)
    Unknown, 35; (3) Emma
    Williams, 35; (4) Christina
    Helberg, 119; night flight, 92;
    pastoral charges: East Saginaw,
    Michigan, 32– Exeter, Ont.,
    24– Glen Mary, Tennessee, 33–
    Harriman, Tennessee, 33–
    Kanyenga Mission, Ont., 27–
    Lapeer, Michigan, 31– Midland,
    Michigan, 32– New Whatcom,
    Washington, 35– Point Edward
    and Wilderness Brights Grove,
    26– Prince Albert Mission, 25–
    Saginaw Valley Convocation
    Missionary, 32– St. Saviour's
    Church, Tollington Park,
    London, England, 41, 108–
    Teeswater, Ont., 27– Wingham,
    Ont., 27– Woodstock, Ont., 24;
    Socialist, 132; true colonizer,
    142; visit to Bairds, 19
Barr, Janette, 125
Barr, John (Jack), 15, 23, 56,
    74-75, 77, 86, 88, 93, 104, 111-
    112, 141

Doukhobors, 2
Dry Farming Congress, 120
Dungannon, 15-16, 20

EASTER MONDAY, 64
Edmonton, 49, 103, 105, 138
Elder Dempster (Beaver Line)
Co., 50, 54, 57
English church, 17-18
Ervin, Ephraim, 12
Ervin, Jane, 12
Esquesing Township, 11-13
Exeter, Ont., 24

FALL OF MAN, The, 27
Ferndale, Washington, 120
Fires, prairie, 81, 142
Flamank, George, 52, 61, 87, 99,
109, 113
Flying Scotsman, 68
Ford family, 12
Forget, Lieutenant-Governor, 73,
134
Forrest, David, 12
Fort Ellice, 25
Fort Garry, 24-25
Fortnightly Review, 42
Fort Pitt, 90, 105
Fox, Mrs., 21
Freighters, 56, 138

GODERICH, Ont., 15
Good Friday, 63-64
Gorriem, Ont., 27
Grace Church, Lapeer, Michigan,
31
Grange, The, 120
Greece, 37
Green, David, 16-17
Green, Gavin Hamilton, 16
Griffin, M. S., 98
Guelph Agricultural College, 57

HALL, Herbert, 57, 84, 103
Halton County, 8-9, 11, 13
Helberg, Christian, 106
Helberg, Christina (Barr), 52,
87-88, 99, 114-118, 120-121,
123-124, 127, 131
Helberg, Mrs. Johanna, 116
Hellmuth, Bishop Isaac, 22, 26,
28-29, 119
Hemstreet family, 12
Hewitt's Landing, 104-105
Hill, Dean Jeffrey, 27-28, 30
Hogan, Mr., 131
Homestead regulations, 50, 89

Hornby, Ont., 9, 11-12, 14
Horses, 102, 137
Hudson's Bay Company, 52
Huguenots, 12
Huron College, 20, 22-23
Hurst, Canon John, 7, 22, 108-109

IMMIGRANTS: German, 48; Polish,
48; Ukrainian, 48
Indians, 52, 62, 77, 82, 103, 107

JONES, Nathaniel, 95-96, 104

KANYENGA MISSION, 27
Kellogg's, Colborne Street, 14
Kelowna, British Columbia, 3
King Edward VII, coronation of,
43, 136
Knox College, Toronto, 9

LADY ELGIN, 14
Lake Manitoba, SS, 5, 53, 58-59,
110, 116; Jackson, ship's packer,
66, 141; passenger list, 83;
steerage, 60
Lake Simcoe, SS, 57
Lapeer County, State of Michigan,
119
Laurie, P. G., 103
Laurier, Sir Wilfrid, 42, 47, 102
Lincoln, Nebraska, 119
Lindsay family, 12
Lindsay, Michael, 11
Ling fish, 60
Liquor and licence, 106-107
Liverpool, 12, 22, 59
Lloyd, George Exton, announces
town of Lloydminster, 105;
appearance, 61; Archdeacon of
Saskatchewan, 107, 112; arrives
at Battleford, 94; Bishop of
Saskatchewan, 107-108;
chaplain, 2, 6, 143; Colonial
and Continental Church Society,
53, 95; colonists turn to, 62-63;
Committee of Twelve, 95, 106,
113; death, 110; director of the
British Colony, 95; first meeting
with Barr, 45; in charge of
colony scheme, 52; leader:
agrees to take over, 65, and
assumes leadership, 80; leaves
Lloydminister, 107; letters to
press, 45; liquor and drinking,
67, 106-107; meeting of
colonists, Battleford, 95;
memoirs, *The Trail of 1903*, 108,

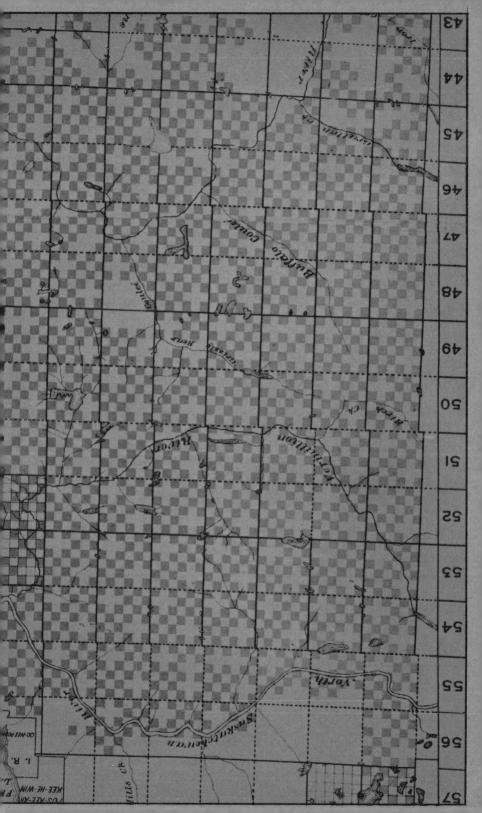